NEW DIRECTIONS FOR COMMUNITY COLLEGES

Arthur M. Cohen   Florence B. Brawer
EDITOR-IN-CHIEF   *ASSOCIATE EDITOR*

Paula Zeszotarski
PUBLICATION COORDINATOR

The New Vocationalism in Community Colleges

Debra D. Bragg
University of Illinois at Urbana-Champaign

EDITOR

Number 115, Fall 2001

JOSSEY-BASS
A Wiley Company
www.josseybass.com

Clearinghouse for Community Colleges

THE NEW VOCATIONALISM IN COMMUNITY COLLEGES
Debra D. Bragg (ed.)
New Directions for Community Colleges, no. 115
Volume XXX, number 3
Arthur M. Cohen, Editor-in-Chief
Florence B. Brawer, Associate Editor

New Directions for Community Colleges is indexed in Current Index to Journals in Education (ERIC).

Microfilm copies of issues and articles are available in 16mm and 35mm, as well as microfiche in 105mm, through University Microfilms Inc., 300 North Zeeb Road, Ann Arbor, Michigan 48106-1346.

ISSN 0194-3081   electronic ISSN 1534-2891   ISBN 0-7879-5780-1

NEW DIRECTIONS FOR COMMUNITY COLLEGES is part of The Jossey-Bass Higher and Adult Education Series and is published quarterly by Jossey-Bass, 989 Market Street, San Francisco, California 94103-1741, in association with the ERIC Clearinghouse for Community Colleges. Periodicals postage paid at San Francisco, California, and at additional mailing offices. POSTMASTER: Send address changes to New Directions for Community Colleges, Jossey-Bass, 989 Market Street, San Francisco, California 94103-1741.

SUBSCRIPTIONS cost $66.00 for individuals and $142.00 for institutions, agencies, and libraries. Prices subject to change.

THE MATERIAL in this publication is based on work sponsored wholly or in part by the Office of Educational Research and Improvement, U.S. Department of Education, under contract number ED-99-CO-0010. Its contents do not necessarily reflect the views of the Department or any other agency of the U.S. Government.

EDITORIAL CORRESPONDENCE should be sent to the Editor-in-Chief, Arthur M. Cohen, at the ERIC Clearinghouse for Community Colleges, University of California, 3051 Moore Hall, Box 951521, Los Angeles, California 90095-1521. All manuscripts receive anonymous reviews by external referees.

Cover photograph © Rene Sheret, After Image, Los Angeles, California, 1990.

Printed in the United States of America on acid-free recycled paper containing 100 percent recovered waste paper, of which at least 20 percent is postconsumer waste.

CONTENTS

EDITOR'S NOTES

Vocational education has been an integral part of community college education since the early twentieth century. Indeed, Lange wrote in *School and Society* in 1918 that "probably the greatest and certainly the most original contribution to be made by the junior college is the creation of [a] means of training for the vocations occupying the middle ground between those of the artisan type and the professions" (p. 213). Particularly since the Truman Commission report in 1947, vocational education has taken on greater prominence within the mission of community colleges, but what is meant by vocational education today is a far cry from the view of post–World War II educators. Even since federal funding first became available to support postsecondary vocational education programs in the Vocational Education Act of 1963, significant changes have occurred in policy and practice at all levels. The current focuses of vocational education present an expanded vision of the field, broadening its impact with external constituents in the community but also extending its influence throughout the K–16 educational system.

The chapters in this volume of *New Directions for Community Colleges* are intended to inform community college educators about changes in policy and practice related to vocational education. Perspectives on these changes are provided by leading researchers and practitioners in the field. Chapter One offers insights into the meaning of the new vocationalism by discussing the context for change, principles that drive the new vocationalism, and threats to its continued survival. In this chapter, I examine efforts of the past decade to integrate vocational education better into the broader agenda of American higher education, including efforts to encourage student transfer and upward mobility. However, challenges still exist because vestiges of the past remain. Even when change is occurring, a lack of knowledge about change perpetuates past beliefs and misconceptions about vocational education today.

Subsequent chapters offer insights into the dimensions of new vocationalism. Michael D. Summers reflects in Chapter Two on the changes that have occurred in vocational education during the past decade as he discusses the emerging role of community college leaders in seeking out and supporting the new vocationalism. Specifically, the chapter provides strategies that local leaders use to address, enhance, and improve vocational education in the community college. In Chapter Three, W. Norton Grubb discusses the policy background to community colleges' expanding role in workforce development. The chapter touches on several dimensions of systemic change linked to workforce and economic development. In Chapter

Four, Margaret Terry Orr discusses new partnerships that are developing between community colleges and their communities. She explores the wide-ranging partnerships and collaborations that community colleges are building to support the new vocationalism. In Chapter Five, Carrie H. Brown presents key components of tech prep. She examines in depth the role that community colleges play in tech prep, with numerous examples of practical strategies that community colleges employ to make tech prep a viable avenue for assisting more students to move successfully from secondary to postsecondary education.

In Chapter Six, Barbara K. Townsend, a leading expert on transfer education, discusses the blurring lines between the age-old notion of terminal education and transfer education. Her chapter describes the increasing prevalence of transfer of vocational students. Using her recent research involving articulation agreements, policies, and practices, Townsend discusses the role that vocational education plays in the reverse-transfer process, that is, the movement of students from four-year to two-year institutions. George H. Johnston, in Chapter Seven, shares local findings concerning work-based learning and compares these results to a national study of work-based learning carried out in ten vocational programs in eight community colleges in the United States. Factors believed to influence successful practice were revisited in 2000, deepening our understanding of what makes for exemplary work-based learning in the two-year college environment. In Chapter Eight, Donna E. Dare focuses on the changing instructional practices that are being employed to serve community colleges' changing student populations better. Practical examples illustrate how colleges are changing vocational education to meet learner needs.

James Jacobs furthers our understanding of the relationships between education and work in his discussion of the role of community colleges in the Workforce Investment Act (WIA), offering some specific examples of how colleges can use this legislation. His chapter offers cautions about problems that lie ahead for dealing with the new buzzword *low-income workers*. The relationship of WIA to programs funded by the Carl D. Perkins Vocational and Technical Education Act of 1998 is explored, including implications for the relationships between secondary and postsecondary vocational-technical education. Finally, Chapter Ten, by Jung-sup Yoo, provides a collection of resources addressing aspects of modern vocational education to assist readers with information about changing policy and practice.

Debra D. Bragg
Editor

Reference

Lange, A. "The Junior College—What Manner of Child Shall This Be?" *School and Society,* 1918, 7, 211–126.

DEBRA D. BRAGG is an associate professor and director of the Office of Community College Research and Leadership at the University of Illinois at Urbana-Champaign (UIUC) and site director for the National Centers for Career and Technical Education at UIUC.

1

Vocational education assumes greater importance as community colleges expand their mission to address growing workforce, economic, and community needs. This chapter provides definitions, principles, and models to illuminate the meaning and importance of the new vocationalism in American community colleges.

Opportunities and Challenges for the New Vocationalism in American Community Colleges

Debra D. Bragg

The mission of community colleges is evolving because the communities within which they are situated are changing. Today's community colleges undertake a number of different functions in an attempt to meet the wide-ranging needs of their constituents. Transfer and liberal arts, vocational education, continuing education and community services, and remedial and developmental education are central to the mission of comprehensive community colleges (Cohen and Brawer, 1996). Some of these functions were evident decades ago when junior colleges originated, but others emerged as the needs of students, employers, schools, universities, community groups, and other entities multiplied and diversified. Undoubtedly, the purpose and role of postsecondary vocational education have changed as well in terms of traditional vocational preparation and with respect to new goals for and approaches to curriculum and instruction. Modern community colleges have a major responsibility for preparing the nation's current and future midskilled workforce, which accounts for three-fourths of all employees in the United States (Grubb, 1996). To address the needs of this segment of the labor force and respond proactively to new economic forces, community colleges provide an array of programs and services. These range from initiatives that link secondary to postsecondary education through tech prep and school-to-work transition programs for the emerging workforce, to certification, licensure, and associate degree programs for incumbent technical workers (Kantor, 1997; Warford and Flynn, 2000).

Today, community colleges face new opportunities and challenges with respect to vocational education. The future is determined, to some extent, by the historic role that vocational education has played in community colleges, but also by recent changes that have attempted to transform the field at both the secondary and postsecondary levels. In this chapter, I explore the meaning of the new vocationalism by defining the concept, describing core principles and exemplars of successful postsecondary initiatives, and examining perennial criticisms. New approaches to vocational education can be designed to prepare learners for meaningful employment and educational experiences that range from immediate entry-level employment to career pathways that require further formal education and lifelong learning.

The New Vocationalism Defined

Many terms have been used to describe postsecondary vocational education over the years, among them such labels as *occupational, career, technical* or *technological, semiprofessional, subbaccalaureate,* and *terminal,* with each of these labels having a slightly different but admittedly related intent. In attempting to sort out the unique meaning of these words, Cohen and Brawer (1996) pointed to the historic significance associated with them, such as the attachment of the *terminal* and *semiprofessional* labels to vocational education in the 1940s and the introduction of career and occupational education in the 1970s. More recently, Grubb (1996) has referred to two-year college degree programs as subbaccalaureate, focusing much of his perspective on vocational education. And technical and technological education came into prominence during the 1990s as tech prep and other forms of technical education moved to center stage (Hershey, Silverberg, Owens, and Hulsey, 1998). All of these labels continue in use in the literature.

During the 1990s, a new set of terminology came into vogue. *Workforce preparation, workforce development, human resource development,* and *economic development* were terms associated with different aspects of vocational education, but typically they were more broadly defined than earlier conceptions. In fact, these labels were sometimes used to distinguish newer education and training programs (such as contract training) from more traditional vocational education. Overall, the intent of programs associated with these ideas was to engage learners in education and training linked to enhancing individual and organizational performance (productivity) in the workplace. *Workforce preparation* is most closely associated with education for the emergent workforce (predominantly traditional college-age learners), whereas *workforce development* and *human resource development* are more closely associated with education and training for incumbent workers and those seeking to upgrade their skills or change careers. *Workforce development* and *human resource development* are also associated routinely with training for a particular organization. Finally, *economic development* refers to the collective programs and services that community colleges carry out to stabilize or increase employment in a community (Grubb and others, 1997). Grubb and others (1997) describe various activities aligned with but independent of education and training as pivotal to economic development, such as technology transfer and economic environmental scanning.

Noting this emerging terminology, I have chosen to focus discussion in this volume using the term *vocational education* because of its longevity and historic significance. In fact, *vocational education* was the term used in the first federal legislation authorizing secondary vocational education programs near the beginning of the twentieth century, under the Smith-Hughes Act of 1917. Respecting this fact and intentionally wanting to cast a wide net to discuss contemporary and future changes, the term *vocational education* is used throughout the volume to provide consistency among chapters and establish a logical benchmark for assessing change from the past to the present and to the future.

Core Principles of the New Vocationalism

During the 1990s, the United States experienced an important shift in public policy, theory, and practice associated with vocational education. The stage for this change was set during prior decades when vocational enrollments increased within community colleges as student populations diversified, secondary schools increasingly struggled to meet the needs of all learners, and the new economy unfolded (Carnevale, 2000; Cohen and Brawer, 1996; Parnell, 1985). Much of the change in vocational education over the past decade or more has gone unheralded, especially by scholars who minimize the importance of community college education, and the vocational function in particular. Yet educators concerned about improving vocational education have attempted to conceptualize new approaches—building on theory, research, and practice—to make improvements in programs and practices. Although change has not come easily, progress has been made, and preliminary results are suggesting important benefits for learners. What changes have been attempted to improve vocational education? What core principles have been supported under the banner of the new vocationalism? What outcomes are anticipated or evident thus far?

First and foremost, the new vocationalism emphasizes career clusters or pathways that extend from the entry level to the professional level in career fields integral to the new economy. Carnevale (2000) labels today's changing labor market the "new economy" because of a proliferation of jobs at the subbaccalaureate level (p. 3), and he envisions community colleges as the nation's primary provider of education and training to meet future workforce needs. Careers in business, health care, and technological fields require technical skills and knowledge, and preparation for these fields occurs largely in subbacalaureate vocational programs. Indeed, the new vocationalism focuses on employment "characterized by international activity, cyberspace, ever-changing market demands and standards, rapid product life cycle, ever-increasingly sophisticated computers and [the] need for a more thorough knowledge of the holistic (the gestalt) of the business environment rather than just specific skills or narrow job tasks" (Lynch, 2000, p. 162). Work in this new environment requires a heightened ability to manage information and technology, analyze and solve problems, and continuously engage in learning to use new and updated information. This picture of the workplace stands in stark contrast to the past, when vocational education was characterized as mostly preparation for narrowly defined, entry-level employment.

Second, understanding the changing nature of modern work provides an important backdrop for understanding the importance of changing and enhancing vocational curriculum. Nearly all modern work requires an integration of academic and technical concepts to solve real-world problems. Therefore, integrated academic and vocational curriculum and instruction is crucial to the preparation of successful employees and lifelong learners. To integrate academic and vocational education effectively, several elements are needed. First, there must be a continuum of vocational preparation (and content) from the general to the specific, and this continuum should start with career exploration beginning at the secondary level or below and move on to more occupationally specific education at the postsecondary level. To avoid this continuum's replicating previous problems with school tracking, integrated instruction should hinge on a comprehensive career cluster or pathway approach that integrates occupations vertically (for example, technician, engineer, scientist) rather than delineates them horizontally (for example, plumber, carpenter, electrician). The curriculum should also emphasize all aspects of the industry, so that students learn how families of occupations are organized and related to one another. This emphasis clearly creates the breadth needed to prepare students for careers, not just immediate entry-level jobs. The U.S. Department of Education's Office of Vocational and Adult Education (OVAE) demonstrates this intent in its effort to redefine vocational education under a new rubric of sixteen career clusters referred to as *building linkages*. In this project, OVAE seeks to link vocational education to a logical categorization of all the jobs in the U.S. labor market.[1]

Third, efforts to implement the new vocationalism are deeply rooted in an attempt to ensure that vocational education is more highly integrated into the K-16 educational system and into broader economic and social structures (Grubb and others, 1999; Orr and Bragg, 2001). Efforts directed at streamlining various vocational education and training programs have proliferated at the state and local levels throughout the nation, and these efforts are directed at ensuring a more logical, systematic, and effective approach to the overall vocational enterprise. To ensure that the breadth of new vocational curriculum is expanded, offering opportunities for advancement in education and employment, the new vocationalism emphasizes career ladders connected to continuing educational opportunities. Integrated academic and vocational curriculum that begins in high school and extends to the two-year-college level, such as tech prep, career academies, youth apprenticeships, middle colleges, and other such options, proliferates as a means of creating linked educational and career pathways. Matriculation from two-year to four-year colleges is increasingly important to advance in career areas that are expanding in the new economy, such as health services, information technologies, and education, and new vocational programs are being designed to address these needs through sequential (seamless) curriculum models. Emerging applied baccalaureate degree programs provide opportunities for students to continue from the two- to the four-year-college level, offering expanded employment opportunities and economic outcomes for students who complete these programs.

Fourth, the new vocationalism encourages constructivist theories, active teaching strategies, and learner-centered, project-based instructional approaches. Learners with a variety of goals and experiences can be prepared in the breadth and depth of knowledge and skills to enable them to succeed in current or future employment and more advanced education and training. Furthermore, learning in nontraditional settings connected to classroom instruction is central to the new vocationalism. Work-based learning (WBL) provides an avenue to assist students in making connections between the theories they learn in class and the work in which they engage in the community. Meaningful linkages between academic and vocational education become viable through experiential learning activities such as WBL. More student-centered learning opportunities are needed to complement traditional teacher-dominated pedagogies (Grubb, 1997, 1999).

Finally, as curriculum and instruction become more meaningful, an increasing number of students can benefit from vocational education. Although postsecondary vocational enrollments are extensive, many individuals are not ready to engage successfully in postsecondary programs. The new vocationalism needs to respond to address the aspirations of students who want to participate in postsecondary education and are needed to work in the new economy, which requires skills and knowledge beyond the high school level (Carnevale, 2000). Sporadic patterns of student enrollment and completion make it difficult to create sequential core curriculum, demanding new models and approaches to curriculum design and delivery. Highly flexible learner-focused approaches to teaching and learning, including using educational technologies, distance learning, and the Internet, need to be developed to address the needs of learners who engage in vocational education. Clearly, in the design of the new vocationalism at the postsecondary level, one size (and one model) will not fit all. For all students, attention must be paid to establishing high-quality instructional programs and ensuring that students meet high standards of academic and occupational performance.

New Models, Approaches, and Initiatives

The five initiatives described in this section point to the breadth and depth of change occurring in vocational education and identify some critical issues pertaining to reforming vocational education within community colleges.

Tech Prep. In 1990, federal vocational education legislation authorized implementation of tech prep through Title IIIE, the Tech Prep Education Act. Established to support a multitude of goals and learner needs, tech prep is intended to establish formal articulation agreements identifying rigorous academic and vocational programs of study having a logical progression from the secondary to the postsecondary level. Through at least a 2+2 sequential curriculum (or additional years of education before or after the 2+2), tech prep should prepare students for college who might not pursue careers requiring postsecondary-level math, science, and technological studies. Several national studies (Boesel, Rahn, and Deich, 1994; Bragg, Layton, and Hammons, 1994; Bragg and others, 1997, 1999) show advancement in tech prep implementation over the 1990s. Considering most programs began planning tech prep in 1991 or later, it is notable that over two-thirds of all U.S. school districts served nearly all secondary students in the nation. Virtually all two-year community, junior, and technical colleges were involved, though student participation was less evident at the postsecondary level (Hershey, Silverberg, Owens, and Hulsey, 1998). Especially at the postsecondary level, implementation issues have emerged with the implementation of tech prep programs. Although many community colleges play a facilitative role, relatively few have accepted far-reaching goals that support systemic reform across the secondary and postsecondary levels.

Work-Based Learning Programs. In addition to the Tech Prep Education Act, other legislation has had a facilitative effect on the new vocationalism, specifically the School-to-Work Opportunities Act of 1994 (STWOA). Key goals of STWOA include secondary-to-postsecondary articulation to enhance transition to college, business partnerships to enhance curriculum development, WBL opportunities, and systemic changes in coordination to enhance educational and economic benefits for all students. At the secondary level, WBL has expanded under STWOA through the establishment of youth apprenticeship programs and cooperative education (co-op), internships, and work study. WBL saw a similar revitalization at the postsecondary level during the 1990s, though on a more modest scale. Still, nearly 20 percent of students in postsecondary vocational programs are estimated to participate in WBL in a wide range of occupational fields (Bragg, Hamm, and Trinkle, 1995). Virtually all community colleges that offer health programs offer WBL opportunities, typically using intensive professional and clinical models. Challenges to offering more WBL relate to the high cost of these programs, difficulties in coordinating WBL for adult students who already hold jobs, and waning commitment by employers over the long term, keeping the pool of students who are likely to benefit quite small and relatively select.

Articulated Vocational Education and Applied Baccalaureate Degree Programs. Long associated with a terminal goal, traditional vocational programs are shedding their dead-end image by encouraging the transfer option (Townsend, 1999). No doubt difficulties exist in transferring credits for students completing vocational programs, because credits associated with vocational courses often do not transfer. However, national studies (Cohen and Ignash, 1994; Prager, 1988) suggest that more vocational students than in the past are choosing to enroll in two-year vocational programs and then transferring to four-year colleges (especially regional public universities, small private colleges, and proprietary colleges offering bachelor's degrees). Known as applied baccalaureate degree programs, transfer is often facilitated through inverted or upside-down degree plans that ensure that technical course work at the two-year level is sequenced with substantial academic course work and more advanced technical courses, frequently referred to as capstone courses, at the university level. Efforts to establish sequential curriculum to assist learners in matriculating from secondary schools to two-year to four-year colleges, a truly intriguing idea, are often met with strong resistance. Misalignment in curriculum content and academic standards is evident across levels, and these gaps and inefficiencies are not entirely haphazard (Orr and Bragg, 2001). Tracking at the secondary level and selectivity at the postsecondary level are built into the system to regulate the flow of students into higher education and the labor market, creating inequities in access and outcomes for all students (Nora, 2000). Nora argues that these inequities have the most negative impact on minority students. Although interest is growing nationwide, few applied baccalaureate degree programs have been implemented in four-year colleges (Southern Illinois University is an exception), and only a few states (one of them is Maryland) have designed policies to facilitate them.

Certification for Credit and Noncredit. Whereas formal collegiate credentials remain important, some argue that skills are equally (and maybe more) important in the new economy (Carnevale, 2000). New certificate programs, typically of eighteen- to twenty-four credit hours, are popping up in community colleges nationwide as they bundle new and existing courses into skill-based certificate packages (Perez and Copenhaver, 1998). Skills associated with information technologies are probably the hottest area now, but certification is growing in other fields, such as health care and business. Often these programs are offered in flexible formats, condensing course work that could take months into a few weeks. In *Faces of the Future,* Phillippe and Valiga (2000) postulate that noncredit enrollments are rising precipitously, and they portray noncredit students as more diverse than credit-seeking students. Specifically, noncredit students represent a broader range of ages and are more likely to have taken previous college courses or hold a bachelor's degree. At the same time, noncredit students are more likely than credit-seeking students to be low income and seeking immediate employment. Phillipe and Valiga conclude that the high level of diversity among noncredit students is "a reflection of non-credit programming offered by community colleges: from training contracted directly by business and industry, to computer training, to personal-enrichment courses, to English-as-a-Second-Language (ESL) and General Educational Development

(GED) courses" (p. 7). No doubt the new economy has had a strong influence on the diversity of students seeking noncredit offerings, and in this phenomenon lies potential conflict for community colleges. The extent to which community colleges will venture away from age-old higher education traditions and reengineer curriculum to meet the immediate economic needs of businesses and industries in their communities is a difficult question. However, it is a question that more and more community colleges are struggling with.

Contract and Customized Training Programs. Sometimes linked to traditional vocational curricula but increasingly tied to continuing education and community services, many community colleges engage in a host of partnership arrangements specifically designed for local business and industry. Grubb and others (1997) characterize this activity as central to the "entrepreneurial" college (p. ix). Indeed, firm-specific contract and customized training is an increasingly important form of the new vocationalism, and it is tightly linked to credit and noncredit certification. Certainly, being more customer focused, responsive, and flexible is indicative of what new workforce and human resource development initiatives are about. These entrepreneurial initiatives are proliferating because they bring in additional revenues to the college, provide greater visibility, meet learner needs for certification and employment, and support the new economy. But in meeting these goals, there is a downside. Grubb and others (1999) caution that entrepreneurial initiatives can splinter vocational efforts from the rest of the college curriculum, diminishing opportunities to develop truly integrated academic and vocational curricula that respond to the broader educational needs of individuals and community societal issues.

Addressing the Critics

Certainly for the critics, the new vocationalism has happened without fanfare. Much like the critics of K–12 education, community college critics have blamed vocational education for tracking students away from the transfer function, thereby squelching opportunity for upward mobility (Brint and Karabel, 1989; Pincus, 1986; Zwerling, 1986). According to the critics, prior efforts to differentiate curriculum (vocational or terminal, liberal arts or transfer) and target specialized programs for needy students or form customized services for business partners have resulted in inequitable outcomes. In fact, vocational education is charged with fulfilling the policy agenda of the privileged elite (Dougherty, 1994). The fact that transfer enrollments for minority students are lower in community colleges that offer extensive vocational programs is further evidence of tracking and inequitable educational opportunity and outcomes (Nora, 2000). With little accumulated research evidence, claims of the penalties associated with participation in postsecondary vocational education are not surprising. Unfounded assertions about the benefits of postsecondary vocational education are equally disturbing. To move forward, both sides require more meaningful results to help distinguish fact from fiction.

Based on an extensive meta-analysis of the literature, Grubb (1998) refuted criticisms of postsecondary vocational education: "Completion of associate degrees enhances wages, employment, and earnings by significant amounts, in both conventional and statistical senses. For example, men with associate degrees earn 18 percent more and women 22.8 percent more than high school graduates, once all the differences between the two groups have been considered" (p. 10). Grubb (1999) has also reported that for minority students who do persist, attending a community college confers greater advantages in the labor market than for whites, compared to high school graduates. These results suggest real economic benefits over a lifetime for community college graduates compared to high school graduates.

Boesel and Fredland (1999) have shown that these benefits extend to students who drop out of four-year colleges. In fact, these economic benefits appear to be distributed fairly equally to all members of the student population or possibly even more so to minority students, though more conclusive research is needed for particular minority groups. Recognizing these benefits, Boesel and Fredland concluded that community colleges make a very important contribution to the future of many high school graduates. Indeed, they recommend an expanded role for community colleges nationally, arguing that they should offer a greater variety of continuing-education and training programs and play a more active role in developing articulated curriculum within elementary and secondary schools to raise the skill levels of high school graduates.

Considering Future Possibilities

As community colleges chart their future, it is important to remember their unique history within America's educational landscape. From almost the start, community colleges have endeavored to serve many masters equally well, but particularly two. They have tried to serve universities through a strong transfer function while also attempting to provide a viable vocational function to fulfill the needs of local employers. Although both functions are important, each has received substantial criticism, particularly vocational education. Over much of the twentieth century, arguments for and against vocational education have been made on political and ideological grounds, but rarely have they been based on empirical results. This is unfortunate because it suggests that community colleges have missed opportunities to steer vocational education in directions that would provide the greatest benefit.

It is important to take stock of postsecondary vocational education and examine its changing focus and evolving goals. Through the collective experiences of community colleges, we may gain insights into how vocational education plays an increasingly prominent role at the postsecondary level and throughout the entire educational system. To be sure, critical questions remain concerning vocational education in community colleges, and these questions need to be addressed through thoughtful research. However, new ideas, models, and approaches are emerging, and these ideas are finding their way into practice. Indeed, these ideas are the foundation for the writing of my fellow authors in this volume. Through our collective observations and insights, we seek to increase understanding about the new vocationalism in U.S. community colleges.

Note

1. See http://www.ed.gov/offices/OVAE/clusters/index.html. Dec. 26, 2000.

References

Boesel, D., and Fredland, E. *College for All*. Washington, D.C.: U.S. Department of Education, National Library of Education, Office of Educational Research and Improvement, 1999.

Boesel, D., Hudon, L., Deich, S., and Masten, C. *Participation in and Quality of Vocational Education, National Assessment of Vocational Education* (Vol. 2). Washington, D.C.: U.S. Department of Education, Office of Educational Research and Improvement, 1994.

Boesel, D., Rahn, M., and Deich, S. *National Assessment of Vocational Education, Final Report to Congress*, Vol. 2: *Program Improvement: Education Reform*. Washington, D.C.: U.S. Department of Education, Office of Educational Research and Improvement, 1994.

Bragg, D. D., Hamm, R. E., and Trinkle, K. A. *Work-Based Learning in Two-Year Colleges in the United States*. Berkeley: National Center for Research in Vocational Education, University of California at Berkeley, 1995.

Bragg, D., Layton, J., and Hammons, F. *Tech Prep Implementation in the United States: Promising Trends and Lingering Challenges*. Berkeley: National Center for Research in Vocational Education, University of California, Berkeley, 1994.

Bragg, D. D., and others. *Tech Prep/School to Work Partnerships: More Trends and Challenges*. Berkeley: National Center for Research in Vocational Education, University of California at Berkeley, 1997.

Bragg, D. D., and others. *Tech Prep Implementation and Preliminary Outcomes for Eight Local Tech Prep Consortia*. Berkeley: National Center for Research in Vocational Education, University of California at Berkeley, 1999.

Brint, S., and Karabel, J. *The Diverted Dream: Community Colleges and the Promise of Educational Opportunity in America, 1900–1985*. New York: Oxford University Press, 1989.

Carnevale, A. P. *Community Colleges and Career Qualifications*. Washington, D.C.: American Association of Community Colleges, 2000.

Cohen, A., and Brawer, F. *The American Community College*. (3rd ed.) San Francisco: Jossey-Bass, 1996.

Cohen, A., and Ignash, J. M. "An Overview of the Total Credit Curriculum." In A. M. Cohen (ed.), *Relating Curriculum and Transfer*. New Directions for Community Colleges, no. 86. San Francisco: Jossey-Bass, 1994.

Dougherty, K. J. *The Contradictory College: The Conflicting Origins, Impacts, and Future of the Community College*. Albany: State University of New York Press, 1994.

Grubb, W. N. *Working in the Middle: Strengthening Education and Training for the Mid-Skilled Labor Force*. San Francisco: Jossey-Bass, 1996.

Grubb, W. N. "Not There Yet: Prospects and Problems for 'Education Through Occupations.'" *Journal of Vocational Education Research,* 1997, 22, 77–94.

Grubb, W. N. *Learning and Earning in the Middle: The Economic Benefits of Sub-Baccalaureate Education.* New York: Community College Research Center, Teachers College, Columbia University, Sept. 1998.

Grubb, W. N. *Honored But Invisible.* New York: Routledge, 1999.

Grubb, W. N., and others. *Workforce, Economic and Community Development: The Changing Landscape of the Entrepreneurial Community College.* Mission Viejo, Calif.: League for Innovation in the Community College, 1997.

Grubb, W. N., and others. *Toward Order from Chaos: State Efforts to Reform Workforce Development "Systems."* Berkeley: National Center for Research in Vocational Education, University of California at Berkeley, 1999.

Hershey, A. M., Silverberg, M. K., Owens, T., and Hulsey, L. K. *Focus for the Future. The Final Report of the National Tech Prep Evaluation.* Princeton, N.J.: Mathematica Policy Research, 1998.

Kantor, S. "Rethinking the Role of Instruction for Workforce Training." In T. Zeiss (ed.), *Developing the World's Best Workforce.* Washington, D.C.: American Association of Community Colleges, 1997.

Lynch, R. "High School Career and Technical Education for the First Decade of the Twenty-First Century." *Journal of Vocational Education,* 2000, 25, 155–198.

Nora, A. *Reexamining the Community College Mission.* Washington, D.C.: American Association of Community Colleges, 2000.

Orr, M. T., and Bragg, D. D. "Policy Directions for K–14 Education: Looking to the Future." In B. Townsend and S. Twombly (eds.), *Educational Policy in the 21st Century,* Vol. 2: *Community Colleges: Policy in the Future Context.* Norwood, N.J.: Ablex, 2001.

Parnell, D. *The Neglected Majority.* Washington, D.C.: Community College Press, 1985.

Perez, S. A., and Copenhaver, C. C. "Certificates on Center Stage: Occupational Education for a Working Economy." *Leadership Abstracts,* 1998, 11, 1–4.

Phillippe, K. A., and Valiga, M. J. *Faces of the Future: A Portrait of American Community College Students.* Washington, D.C.: American Association of Community Colleges, 2000.

Pincus, F. "Vocational Education: More False Promises." In L. S. Zwerling (ed.), *The Community College and Its Critics.* New Directions for Community Colleges, no. 53. San Francisco: Jossey-Bass, 1986.

Prager, C. "The Other Transfer Degree." In C. Prager (ed.), *Enhancing Articulation and Transfer.* New Directions for Community Colleges, no. 61. San Francisco: Jossey-Bass, 1988.

Townsend, B. "Reassessing the Transfer Function." Paper presented at the Association for the Study of Higher Education, San Antonio, Tex., Nov. 1999.

Warford, L., and Flynn, W. J. "New Game, New Rules: The Workforce Development Challenge." *Leadership Abstract,* 2000, 13, 1–4.

Zwerling, L. S. (ed.). *The Community College and Its Critics.* New Directions for Community Colleges, no. 54. San Francisco: Jossey-Bass, 1986.

DEBRA D. BRAGG *is an associate professor and director of the Office of Community College Research and Leadership at the University of Illinois at Urbana-Champaign (UIUC) and site director for the National Centers for Career and Technical Education at UIUC.*

2

Vocational education is occurring in an environment of new technologies, global competition, and changing demographics that is transforming community colleges. Leaders with foresight and courage will have a positive influence on their institutions and promote the new vocationalism.

The Role of Leadership in Successful Vocational Initiatives

Michael D. Summers

Vocational-technical education conjures up a variety of images and perceptions based on one's experiences as a student. Many are likely to recall the 1960s and early 1970s as a time when they built birdhouses, candlestick holders, or bookends in high school shop class. Students in the late 1970s and 1980s probably remember the incredible quantity of choices in office and technical programs offered at local community colleges. Students in the 1990s are likely to reminisce about education that saw an increased number of certificates and degrees related to computers, in addition to the numerous programs that were becoming connected to high schools, senior institutions, and employers. Today, community colleges are striving to understand and address the challenges of the new century. How will vocational education be remembered a few decades from now?

Some scholars contend that the latest version of vocational education is already emerging. Called the *new vocationalism* by some while being touted as a myth by others, this latest evolution of vocational education is replete with several noteworthy features, including merging of transfer and terminal curricula, forging complex articulation agreements at multiple levels, and infusing a lifelong perspective in workforce development. Other critical components are an integral part of the new vocationalism, but this chapter focuses on the influence that community college leaders have on this newest version of vocational education.

Influence of Leaders

Considerable differences of opinion exist among scholars and practitioners regarding the influence of a president and senior administrators on the institutional mission and vision of a college. Cohen and March (1974) have

NEW DIRECTIONS FOR COMMUNITY COLLEGES, no. 115, Fall 2001 © John Wiley, & Sons, Inc.

described the presidency as analogous to trying to steer a skidding automobile. Just as a driver has limited control over the direction of the sliding vehicle, they contend that a president has limited influence and control on the overall position of the institution. Birnbaum (1988) has argued that presidents are mistaken if they think they can significantly change an institution. He claims that presidents should strive to illuminate issues instead of deciding them, essentially suggesting that presidents actually accomplish more by directing attention than directing employees. Birnbaum (1992) later argued that because the purposes and goals of an institution are largely shaped by its history, culture, and training of its staff, authoritarian presidential leadership is more likely to cause conflict than desirable outcomes. One could ask whether weak presidential leadership is a significant influence on institutional vision and mission.

Other practitioners and scholars have essentially an opposite view of the influence of presidential leadership. For instance, Rhodes (1998) claims that "the first and greatest task of a president is to articulate the vision, champion the goals, and enunciate the objectives" (p. 14) of the institution. Rhodes says that the president must use his or her skills to "dream the institution into something new, to challenge it to greatness, to elevate its hopes and extend its reach" (p. 14). Rhodes acknowledges that this cannot be accomplished alone. It requires assistance from the management team, colleagues, advisers, and consultants. Parnell (1988) has asserted, "A leader sets the tone, the motivation, and the positive attitudes about the future of an organization or the group that he or she is leading and articulates these clearly as part of the mission and goals of the organization" (p. 1). Moreover, Roueche, Baker, and Rose (1989), after studying fifty prominent community college presidents, found that vision was the most significant theme identified as key to successful leadership.

While I acknowledge the conflicting viewpoints on the potential influence of presidential leadership, it is my belief that community college presidents and their senior administrators have an influence on the mission and vision of an institution and can steer it in a positive direction. This influence is essential for community colleges as they strive to develop and deliver the highest-quality education while supporting the changing scope of vocational education on their campuses.

Essential Leadership Skills: Foresight and Courage

Community college leaders need to leverage specific leadership features if they expect to have a positive influence on the changing scope of vocational education. They can improve their institutions by reinforcing two personal leadership qualities: foresight and courage. The strengthening of these two qualities can have considerable influence on the ability to develop vocational educational initiatives in their community colleges into the new vocationalism that is necessary to meet the demands of the new century.

Foresight. Leadership in community colleges has always involved foresight—that is, looking to the future and anticipating what needs to be done while at the same time being attentive to the many existing needs of individuals and constituency groups. Certainly, a president with any longevity learned early on the importance of being keenly attentive to the board to whom he or she directly reports and understanding the board's future agenda. Moreover, attention to current and upcoming federal and state legislation provides the legal and fiduciary boundaries that shape and guide community college leaders. Furthermore, attention to the existing and future needs of the local community provides a necessary base of support for defining the college's purposes. However, foresight as discussed in this chapter refers to the unwavering commitment of leaders to seek out, listen to, and understand the views, trends, successes, and failures that suggest what a community college should become. Indeed, this view of foresight goes beyond what the board, state legislature, and local community view as future needs. This kind of foresight requires looking for ways to lead an institution, finding new solutions to old problems and new relationships with different groups, and developing new options for students.

Alfred and Carter (1998) contend that community colleges have been successful at responding to the many constituencies they serve, but "their abilities to anticipate future needs of students and identify and develop new markets remain surprisingly weak" (p. 30). The leaders of a community college need to develop a commitment to anticipate and look for ways to develop into an institution that serves more needs and serves more purposes. This kind of leadership has the potential to change vocational education from a nontransferable, limited, workforce supply mission into something much broader. Consider the following examples, where academic leaders focused not only on the challenges of the present but anticipated how their institutions could expand their vocational education programs.

Danville Area Community College. Danville Area Community College (DACC) is a small, rural, public community college located in east-central Illinois serving approximately eighteen hundred full-time-equivalent (FTE) credit students annually. Throughout the 1980s and early 1990s, as this community was recovering from plant closures, downsizing, local unemployment rates as high as 24 percent, and a shrinking district population, the leadership of the college was remarkably proactive and attentive to the future. At a time of declining revenues and shrinking enrollment, the president had the foresight to send teams of college staff in 1996 to England and Germany to study new models of vocational education. The leaders of this institution were convinced that they needed different solutions to address the workforce development problems facing the community, and they saw the exposure to new thinking as an important investment in the future. Concurrently, a special line item was established in the college's annual budget for "best-practice site" visits beyond normal institutional funding for administrator, faculty, and staff travel budgets. This fund was designed to support employee attendance at regional and national conferences and visits to other colleges that had demonstrated successful solutions to problems related to vocational education and economic development (DACC Administrative Council, 1997). The foresight exhibited by these leaders to look beyond the scarce resources and other challenges of the present and concentrate on what needed to be done to position the institution for the future was critical in improving their vocational education.

As a result of these investments, according to the college leaders, several new initiatives were begun that changed the nature and scope of vocational education at DACC. For example, several new apprenticeship programs were developed in the ensuing years, a reorganized Department of Continuing Education was established to meet employee development needs of local companies, new articulation agreements were approved with senior institutions, and liberal arts faculty became more involved in the development and delivery of vocational education at the institution.

All of these activities were the direct result of the foresight of the institutional leaders. These activities expanded vocational education at DACC beyond its original scope. The college's role in economic development evolved to include providing incubator space for new companies, customized employment training for all workers, and unique apprenticeship programs for local machining, manufacturing, and electronics industries. Moreover, transfer articulation agreements in previously nontransferable programs were approved for senior institutions in Illinois and Indiana. Associate in applied science (A.A.S.) graduates in automotive technology, electronics, manufacturing, and computer-aided design were now essentially transfer students if they so desired, ending the stigma of vocational education as being a terminal program. Indeed, these new initiatives greatly expanded the college's partnerships and the overall scope of the vocational enterprise.

Greenville Technical College. Greenville Technical College (GTC), located in the northwestern portion of South Carolina, is a large multicampus, urban public community college that serves more than six thousand FTE credit students annually. It has seen its enrollment grow at an average rate of 5 percent each year for the past five years in spite of a local unemployment rate of approximately 2 percent. Economic development in the upstate region of South Carolina has been nothing short of incredible, with the creation of more than forty-seven thousand new jobs over the past two decades. However, this growth has not prevented leaders at GTC from having the foresight to seek ways to influence programming and the community at large.

College leaders, for example, helped to establish the Charter High School on the GTC campus in 1999 with the expectation of providing a new model for the ultimate partnership between public secondary education and postsecondary technical training (GTC Charter High School Charter Committee, 1998). The GTC Charter High School is the largest of its kind in the state, with funding provided by the South Carolina Department of Education. It is an open, tuition-free institution available to any high school student in Greenville County. The school is designed for four hundred students, with the expectation that its students will enroll in college classes as part of their high school curriculum. Moreover, collaboration between the faculty and staff of the high school and college has led to an integrated curriculum, with the potential of allowing a student to complete a two-year degree concurrently with the course requirements for high school graduation. This unique partnership has expanded the traditional boundaries of articulation and curriculum integration to new levels. The possibility of engaging students in postsecondary vocational and technical training potentially through all four years of their high school experience is not business as usual, reflecting an important dimension of the new vocationalism.

Greenville Tech is also a partner with the Greater Greenville Chamber of Commerce and several local industries, such as Michelin, General Electric, Hitachi, and Bausch & Lomb. Together with the college, these companies established the Upstate Training Alliance in 1998 (Upstate Training Alliance Board of Directors, 1998). This unique program was created to address a possible labor shortage in the multiskilled industrial maintenance field and to provide students the intensive training necessary to succeed in the occupation. The Upstate Training Alliance represents a collaboration of companies that normally compete with each other for top candidates in this technical field. The program, supported with $200,000 in recurring state funding annually, provides free tuition and books, pay and benefits, college credit, and on-the-job training. These programs and services are provided for students selected by the participating companies, which also pay students' costs. The expectation is that those who complete the work will be hired on a full-time basis at the conclusion of the program. This vocational program is supported through a recurring line item in the state's budget, involves several companies in the development and delivery of curriculum, and has initiated a workforce development system that is used in a recruitment package promoted by the local and state chambers of commerce and local and state economic development officials.

Finally, Greenville Tech has worked in partnership with the University of South Carolina and the School District of Greenville County to create a virtual high school for the Fine Arts Center (FAC) of Greenville County in the 2000 academic year. The FAC is South Carolina's first secondary school for gifted and talented students in the literary, visual, and performing arts. It selects students according to talent and provides a unique opportunity to develop that talent and prepare them for entry into college or conservatory programs. (The FAC had approximately three hundred students in attendance for the 1999–2000 school year.) The FAC is a cluster arts magnet program offering arts training at the center; the students who attend take academic courses at their respective county high schools or other school sites.

In yet another example, a collection of high school courses that could be delivered over the Internet and with curriculum based on the South Carolina standards for a high school diploma were identified. Greenville Tech acts as the course provider, delivering a curriculum that is enhanced by integrating the academics with the arts in a project-based environment, culminating in a senior portfolio. Students selecting this option have access to an appropriate accredited curriculum without having to return to their home high school for academic classes. The University of South Carolina is involved in this initiative by engaging in a research project that tracks the virtual students and compares their performance with traditional students.

In all three of these initiatives, the leadership of Greenville Technical College showed the foresight to examine the broader and long-term needs of its community's education system and imagine what it needed to become to assist in meeting those needs. College leaders were willing to search out new solutions to old problems by collaborating and building new partnerships with other institutions and agencies. The scope of vocational education occurring at Greenville Tech goes far beyond conventional practices, illustrating numerous examples of the new vocationalism. Unique articulation, partnerships, and multiple learning settings have pushed the limits of vocational education to include myriad activities new to this community college.

Courage. The second leadership quality or skill that can help a president and senior administrators to expand their influence on vocational education is courage. Leadership is not well suited to the faint of heart, so I am referring to courage in the context of making specific choices and decisions. Munitz (1998) asserts, "Strong executives require courage, a willingness to take risks, an ability to dream about alternatives while weighing their consequences, and the capacity to engage colleagues from different perspectives toward common goals" (p. 9). Community college leaders have a particular need for courage now that many institutions are being asked to do more with limited resources. Indeed, Addy (1995) claims that "every social issue becomes our issue; every educational issue becomes our issue; every economic issue becomes our issue; and every political issue becomes our issue" (p. 134).

Clearly, most community colleges do not have unlimited resources, so they must determine what issues, projects, and initiatives they will take on while maintaining an appropriate level of quality. Gilliland (1995) argues, "Having come from a background of trying to be all things to all people, we are now beginning the process of learning how to sift through the many opportunities and offers that are available to us" (p. 42). Gilliland explains that saying no to a particular project or potential partner is difficult and a new experience for many community college leaders. To be sure, it does call into question an institution's mission and purpose, and it takes courage for leaders to maintain focus. Leaders with the courage to identify inappropriate activities serve their institutions well by maintaining the proper allocation of resources to priority activities. This encourages development in selected areas and provides greater opportunities to improve vocational education in scope and quality.

Leaders at DACC faced a critical decision in 1997 when they had to decide whether to invest scarce resources in the development of a comprehensive on-line program or create a new solution to a local manufacturing labor shortage. The college did not have the personnel, time, or financial resources to undertake both projects with equal speed and resources, so the initiative offering the better opportunity for the college had to be chosen. The institutional leaders had the courage to make a decision, and it proved to be valuable in terms of improving the vocational education offered by the institution.

The leadership of the college was faced with technical training that was insufficient to satisfy employer demands in a changing environment and was challenged to develop a new solution to this workforce development need quickly. College officials accepted the challenge, and a new leading-edge program was designed and implemented that would recruit, train, and provide employment for technically proficient workers for the manufacturing industry. The program, entitled the Fast-Track Apprenticeship Program, provided the opportunity for participants to complete an A.A.S. degree in industrial maintenance in approximately one year, an accelerated pace (Summers and Mills, 1997). Features that made this overall project particularly innovative were that the program did not follow the traditional academic calendar; that it included as an incentive the companies' paying for all of the participants' costs of tuition, fees, and textbooks; that the company employed the participants on a part-time basis while they were enrolled in the program, to complement and apply what was taught in the college courses; and that the participants, assuming they completed the program successfully, were eligible for full-time employment with the company and an opportunity to pursue a number of career paths.

Overall, the Fast-Track Apprenticeship Program offered the college, companies, and community an efficient and effective workforce development strategy that met the immediate and long-term needs of the manufacturing industry. The accelerated pace, integrated part-time employment component, and company-paid incentives created a growing interest in the manufacturing field as a career opportunity for many citizens in the district. Moreover, the success of this program spread to companies in other community college districts in Illinois and Indiana, leading to an expansion of the unique program into surrounding areas. This unforeseen benefit arguably created opportunities for the institution that outweighed those offered by on-line instruction.

The college leadership had the courage to decide on one of the options available at the time, recognizing that they could not adequately pursue both opportunities with equal vigor. By concentrating appropriate resources into the chosen option, they were able to meet and even exceed their expectations.

Conclusion

The leaders in all community colleges today face a daunting array of challenges that provide opportunities for institutions to grow or to atrophy. Vocational education is in the middle of this environment, with the potential to evolve into a more complex category of higher education. This change in the scope of vocational education is occurring in an environment where rapidly accelerating technology, global competition, and changing demographics are creating new types of organizations that were not even imagined a few years ago (Hesselbein, Goldsmith, and Beckhard, 1996). Leaders with foresight and courage can positively influence their institution in ways that will improve vocational education.

Roueche, Baker, and Rose (1989) claimed over a decade ago that "today's leaders, the second generation, must be strong enough to cope with problems of the existing organization and the challenges it faces. We have entered into a new era of leadership in which presidents must develop and communicate their vision, mobilize people in new directions, and convert followers into leaders" (p. 10). We are now into our third generation of community college leaders, and these leaders need to have a full set of skills to meet the challenges facing their institutions. Undoubtedly, foresight and courage are two important skills to have as community colleges move forward.

References

Addy, C. L. *The President's Journey: Issues and Ideals in the Community College.* Bolton, Mass.: Anker Publishing Company, 1995.

Alfred, R., and Carter, P. "Staying Competitive: New Tactics for Organizational Development." *Community College Journal,* 1998, *68,* 30–34.

Birnbaum, R. *How Colleges Work: The Cybernetics of Academic Organization and Leadership.* San Francisco: Jossey-Bass, 1988.

Birnbaum, R. *How Academic Leadership Works: Understanding Success and Failure in the College Presidency.* San Francisco: Jossey-Bass, 1992.

Clark, W., and Elliott, G. *Virtual High School of the Fine Arts Center.* Greenville, S.C.: Greenville Technical College, June 13, 2000.

Cohen, M., and March, J. *Leadership and Ambiguity: The American College President.* New York: McGraw-Hill, 1974.

Danville Area Community College Administrative Council. Meeting minutes, Feb.–June 1997.

Gilliland, J. R. "Community College and Collaboration." In J. E. Roueche, L. S. Taber, and S. D. Roueche (eds.), *The Company We Keep: Collaboration in the Community College.* Washington, D.C.: Community College Press, 1995.

Greenville Technical College Charter High School Charter Committee. "Greenville Technical College Charter High School—Proposal." Greenville, S.C.: Greenville Technical College, July 27, 1998.

Hesselbein, F., Goldsmith, M., and Beckhard, R. (eds.). *The Leader of the Future: New Visions, Strategies, and Practices for the Next Era.* San Francisco: Jossey-Bass, 1996.

Munitz, B. "Leaders: Past, Present, and Future." *Change,* 1998, *30,* 8–9.

Parnell, D. "Leadership Is Not Tidy." *Leadership Abstracts,* 1988, *1,* 1.

Rhodes, F. H. "The Art of the Presidency." *Presidency,* Spring 1998, 12–18.

Roueche, J. E., Baker, G. A., and Rose, R. R. *Shared Vision: Transformational Leadership in American Community Colleges.* Washington, D.C.: Community College Press, 1989.

Summers, M. D., and Mills, D. "Post-Secondary Apprenticeship System Proposal." Danville, Ill.: Danville Area Community College, Dec. 10, 1997.

Upstate Training Alliance Board of Directors. "Upstate Companies Unite to Fill Growing Need." Press release. Greenville, S.C.: Greenville Technical College, May 26, 1998.

MICHAEL D. SUMMERS *is vice president for education at Greenville Technical College, Greenville, South Carolina.*

3

This chapter offers a new vision for vocational education and systems of workforce development covering both education and training to address duplication, waste, and ineffectiveness. By targeting programs on the most promising employment opportunities, education providers can develop integrated systems that yield positive outcomes for students and employers.

From Isolation to Integration: Postsecondary Vocational Education and Emerging Systems of Workforce Development

W. Norton Grubb

What do we, as citizens and employees, policymakers and employers, want of our educational and workforce development systems? That we continue to expand and elaborate education and training, trying various reforms every few years, shows that we clearly want a great deal. Examining these developments is crucial to understanding our ambitions for education and training and understanding the particular role of vocational education within a larger complex of programs. Over the past decade, the former National Center for Research in Vocational Education (NCRVE) at the University of California, Berkeley, conducted numerous studies of the efforts to create more coherent and effective systems of workforce preparation. This chapter summarizes that research.

Background

In the United States, an imposing system of public and private education developed during the nineteenth and twentieth centuries. The term education has usually encompassed a variety of intellectual, political, and moral goals, as well as occupational preparation. The resulting complex of institutions, larger than in any other country, is marked by substantial regularity, with obvious similarities in particular institutions and well-established patterns of progression, from elementary school to high school and college to postgraduate study. Much of the funding for this system is public, even at the postcompulsory level, because access has been a persistent concern. The process of developing our educational

NEW DIRECTIONS FOR COMMUNITY COLLEGES, no. 115, Fall 2001   © John Wiley, & Sons, Inc.

system has been complex, to be sure, but the result of pulling and tugging by millions of citizens, policymakers, and educators is a system of widespread access, considerable transparency, and variation within clear limits.

Over a considerably shorter period of time—little more than three decades—a different system of workforce development has begun to emerge in much the same way, from federal and state support, local experimentation, and considerable wrangling about the results (Grubb, 1996). In contrast to the broader goals of education, this training system has emphasized occupational preparation, often narrowly defined. Its programs are usually shorter, rarely lasting more than fifteen weeks; they are usually open only to specific groups, like the long-term unemployed, dislocated workers, or welfare recipients; they are provided in a bewildering variety of community-based organizations, firms, unions, and proprietary schools as well as educational institutions; and they provide a much greater variety of services than education usually does. Training, as distinct from education, has been largely a federal initiative rather than one from the states. This system is not as settled as formal education has become. Its institutions and programs are more fluid and varied, the linkages among programs are largely undeveloped, and its effects are much less clear. The variations among states and localities are even more substantial than they are in the education system. In many states, a rough system is emerging, but many issues remain unresolved, among them the scope and equity of access, the nature and quality of specific programs, and the patterns of mobility among programs. The process of reform is also uneven and slow; as a policymaker in Oklahoma described the process, "You can't eat an elephant in one bite" (Grubb and others, 1999, p. 2).

Providers of postsecondary vocational education, particularly community colleges and technical institutes, are virtually the only programs that participate in both education and workforce development. Therefore, vocational education has the potential to bridge education and training, providing a route from short-term programs back into the mainstream of education. In some states, community colleges and technical institutes are central to all workforce development, and in a few localities they are "the only game in town." The practices developed in the most progressive vocational programs can provide examples for other programs to emulate, potentially improving the effectiveness of the entire system. But where community colleges and other providers of vocational and adult education have failed to participate in state discussions about workforce development, the cleavage between education and training has persisted, to the detriment of all.

The Growth of the Elephant: The Elaboration of Programs

Workforce development programs provide individuals with the competencies necessary for employment: technical skills; basic academic competencies in remedial and adult education; skills like problem solving, communications, and teamwork, often associated with skills put forth by the Secretary's Commission on Achieving Necessary Skills (SCANS) in 1991; and soft skills like motivation, reliability, and the ability to work with others. A conventional history starts with the manpower programs established by the federal government in the early 1960s to combat technological unemployment and poverty. Setting a pattern that has complicated the system ever since, early manpower programs viewed schools and colleges as inappropriate places to provide short, job-specific training for individuals who had not previously done well in schooling. Services were therefore provided outside the educational system, particularly by community-based organizations, thereby creating the distinction between education and training.

One strand of development includes the elaboration of short-term job training programs, which were consolidated and reformed first in the Comprehensive Employment and Training Act of 1973, then in the Job Training Partnership Act (JTPA) of 1981, and most recently in the Workforce Investment Act (WIA) of 1998. Another strand has focused on welfare recipients, first in the services strategy of the 1960s to enable welfare recipients to find employment and then expanded in various welfare-to-work programs developed during the 1980s. Most recently, the Personal Responsibility and Work Opportunity Reconciliation Act of 1996 has imposed new requirements to move individuals off welfare, reinforcing a strategy of work first, or placing individuals into employment rather than education or training.

Over time, federal legislation has tended to expand the groups eligible for short-term job training to include dislocated workers unemployed because of sectoral shifts, food stamp recipients, those injured on the job and needing vocational rehabilitation, veterans, and a variety of others. And throughout these developments in job training, the federal government has slowly expanded support for adult education as well, providing remedial education and English as a Second Language (ESL). As a result, a confusing array of employment and training programs exists. In 1995, the General Accounting Office counted 163 federal programs spending $20.4 billion. The report *America's Choice: High Skills or Low Wages!* (National Commission on Education and the Economy, 1990) described the problem in these words: "The network of public training activities in this country has thus been created as a result of unrelated education, social, and economic development goals rather than from any overall vision of human resource development. The result is a crazy quilt of competing and overlapping policies and programs, with no coherent system of standardization or information exchange services on which various providers and agencies can rely" (pp. 53–54).

At the same time as federal developments have driven the system, states have elaborated their own programs. Area vocational schools, community colleges and technical institutes, and adult education have expanded substantially since the 1960s. Almost every state has enacted programs supporting training in order to stimulate economic development, often by subsidizing training within firms. Like the federal government, states have found themselves with a plethora of programs, some state initiated and funded and others largely federal.

Complaints About the System: Rhetoric and Reality

As federal and state policymakers have contemplated what they have wrought, similar complaints from each sector have emerged over nearly thirty years (Grubb, Brown, Kaufman, and Lederer, 1989; Grubb and others, 1999; Hollinger and Harvey, 1994). One problem is overlap and duplication. Many programs provide similar services; for example, secretarial, computer-related, and electronics programs are provided by job training and welfare-related programs, as well as community colleges and area vocational schools, and remedial education exists in community colleges, adult education, and learning labs sponsored by job training. Because most programs have been independent of one another, progress from one to another—for example, from adult education for remedial purposes into job training for technical skills, or from a basic computer skills course into a more advanced program providing access to better jobs—has been left to the initiative of students. From the perspective of students and employers, the variety of programs has made it difficult to know which programs are available, which are most effective, and where the most reliable employees might be found. And so charges of limited information, inadequate access, inefficiency, and duplication have proliferated.

Many of the concerns are justified, but in other cases they seem exaggerated. Contrary to conventional wisdom, there are remarkably few cases of outright duplication. One reason is that programs vary in their services, with vocational programs concentrating on longer-term certificate and associate degree programs, while job training and welfare programs emphasize short-term training, on-the-job training (often a wage subsidy rather than real training), and job search assistance. Programs also vary in the individuals they serve, with job training and welfare-to-work programs serving more disadvantaged individuals than community colleges do, and customized training offering training to individuals already employed. An overall shortage of resources means that there is generally more demand than existing programs can supply.

Most communities also have systems of education and training in the sense that many services are available. Virtually every community has a continuum of remediation programs leading to the general equivalency diploma (within adult education) or college-level courses (within community colleges), a variety of job-specific training from short-term entry-level programs in area vocational schools and community-based organizations to two-year associate degree programs in well-paid fields, and ancillary services like job search assistance and placement services.

Again contrary to convention, at the local level there is often considerable coordination (Grubb and McDonnell, 1996; Grubb and Kalman, 1994). Most communities have a system in the sense that administrators of programs are familiar with other programs, and extensive referral and contracting among programs take place. In the most typical pattern, for example, secondary and postsecondary vocational programs are linked by articulation agreements and 2+2 agreements; job training and welfare-to-work programs subcontract with community colleges to provide some (though not all) of their training and remediation, with adult schools usually providing the lion's share of remediation and ESL; and community colleges provide customized training for employers with their own resources, as well as funds from state economic development efforts. Such coordination has often been the result of local initiatives rather than federal requirements or state policies.

In other communities, different patterns of coordination emerge. In one pattern, education programs coordinate with one another, particularly through articulation agreements, and various job training programs have cooperated with one another. Nevertheless, a cleavage persists between education, on the one hand, and training, on the other. Another pattern emerges in the few communities in which the community college is the only game in town. In this situation, the community college may provide not only vocational education of various duration but also adult education, the majority of job training (sometimes in collaboration with community-based organizations), a variety of economic development efforts, and services to employers as well. A few communities have a series of local programs that are potential competitors to one another, where there seems to have been a mutual agreement not to infringe on the territory of others.

Although there is certainly more coordination than the conventional wisdom claims, the dominant view is that the existing systems are not coherent enough. One problem is that there are very few mechanisms for following individuals, helping them make transitions among programs, providing them assistance if they falter, or giving them information about the alternatives available. As a result, referral among programs—for example, from job training to adult education or from a welfare program to a community college—is likely to result in individuals' becoming lost by tracking systems rather than being an effective method of cooperation. One welfare administrator lamented sending clients to "the black hole of adult basic education" (Grubb, Brown, Kaufman, and Lederer, 1989, p. 6); the lack of tracking mechanisms meant that the program never knew whether the individual arrived at the remedial program, completed the program, made it back into job skills training, completed training, and finally managed to find stable employment.

The lack of adequate tracking mechanisms (and then supportive services) is symptomatic of another problem in local systems: the lack of information. Aside from figures on enrollments required for funding, few programs collect data on dimensions of performance like the progress of individuals through various services, completion rates, subsequent employment, and long-term earnings. There is substantial agreement that dropout rates from all programs are high. However, few programs collect such information, and job training providers have often fudged the numbers so that true completion rates cannot be calculated. Community colleges often reinterpret low completion rates as evidence that their students have gotten related employment, without knowing anything about what their students do when they leave, effectively defining away the problem. Results on subsequent employment and earnings are even harder to find, particularly for individual programs. Even in JTPA, which was conventionally thought to be outcome oriented because of its performance standards, local programs tended to be performance driven but not outcome oriented. They often were concerned with meeting specific performance targets but ignorant about other dimensions of success.

Finally, the effectiveness of many programs has been suspect (Grubb, 1996). Sophisticated evaluations reveal that short-term job training tends to increase earnings by trivial amounts—on the average by $200 to $500 per year—and that even these benefits decline over four to five years. Most welfare-to-work programs have failed to move welfare recipients into independent employment, and the results for the most disadvantaged participants are especially disheartening. The periods of time that most individuals enroll in adult education are too short to make much difference, the rates of noncompletion from community colleges have been much too high, and the proportion of completers who find related employment is quite low in many vocational areas. In economic development, the dominant approach of trying to lure industry from neighboring states with various tax and training incentives is rarely effective. Many training efforts funded in the name of economic development provide public subsidies for training that employers would otherwise fund themselves. In effect, the overriding concern with duplication and waste, the focus on specific program requirements, and the lack of information and evaluation have led to systems with remarkably little attention to effectiveness. And so various efforts to improve the quality of programs have emerged: performance standards, required first in JTPA and now spreading to other programs; the development of state data systems to improve information about outcomes; and even performance-based funding, first tried in Florida.

Progress in the States

Before the late 1980s, most successful efforts at coordination were local. Since then, however, states have become increasingly active in defining and coordinating their workforce development programs, sometimes in response to state economic problems, sometimes in recognition that the plethora of programs was unwieldy and ineffective. At least in the most active states, such efforts have had real effects. The results provided in this section are based on examining ten such states (Grubb and others, 1999).

The dominant state strategy is simply described, though it has many variants. A state agency, often called a workforce development (or investment) board, is created with a certain set of statewide responsibilities, usually for planning and oversight of education and training programs, and sometimes with administrative responsibilities as well. Then, because state offices are rarely familiar with local conditions, local or regional counterparts are established with responsibility for implementing state policy. The programs included in these state initiatives vary; they almost always include job training and welfare-to-work programs, as well as recent initiatives like school-to-work programs and one-stop centers; they sometimes include state economic development activities. In some states, postsecondary vocational education and adult education are also included, and in others they have been left out, sometimes because they have fought politically not to be included. Some state councils are advisory; others have administrative powers and can therefore make funding decisions that force collaboration and consolidation.

States have used a variety of other instruments to reform workforce development. Some have stressed institutional mechanisms of change—efforts to improve the quality of programs and the connections among them, including required advisory committees, technical assistance to local programs, and (particularly in the largely voluntary efforts in Oklahoma and Oregon) cultural changes, shifting away from the traditional state role of funding and regulation to one of state leadership with local responsibility. Other states, particularly Florida and Texas, have adopted market-like mechanisms. Performance measures and standards to emphasize outcomes over inputs are one widespread reform. Florida has moved toward performance-based funding; 15 percent of funds for various education and training providers are based on completion of credentials and job placement rates. Increased competition among providers, subcontracting of services, and vouchers are market-like mechanisms used in varying ways.

The state-level developments have not been smooth and easy. Some states, like Oregon, North Carolina, and Florida, have stuck to a basic strategy over relatively long periods of time, and they have made the most progress. But in other states, including Massachusetts and Maryland, changes in administrations have brought in governors with very different political agendas, reversing earlier progress to coordinate programs. In other cases, notably Wisconsin and Michigan, a focus on welfare reform and work first—the philosophy of emphasizing immediate employment as the best route to economic independence—has undermined efforts to develop education and training programs further and alienated employers. As one local official noted, "I don't think that [work first] is doing a service to the employer or to the individual. . . . And if I had that attitude of not wanting to seek retention on the job, I would lose the employers who are the customers of the center—and I can't afford to lose them. The board will fire [us] if we're just throwing bodies at employers" (Grubb and others, 1999, p. 87).

In addition, resistance from some providers, particularly adult education, and inconsistency in state decisions have presented other problems to local efforts at coordination. On the whole, however, many states have become more active in developing their workforce development systems.

At the local level, an important trend has been the creation of one-stop centers, funded by the Department of Labor. In some states, these centers provide information to prospective students (and to employers) about the programs available locally. In other cases, they have moved beyond the provision of information to career-oriented counseling and help in enrollment. Sometimes different programs maintain offices colocated at the one-stop center; in these cases, one-stop centers have become a single point of entry into the workforce development system. Sometimes the process of creating one-stop centers has caused local programs to engage in more extensive cooperation in the provision of services. As a local official in Michigan noted, "No Wrong Door [the one-stop center] is really forcing us all to sit down at the table and figure out how we can maintain a system and still provide what we think are essential services to a universal population with reduced budgets" (Grubb and others, 1999, p. 64).

In addition, the creation of local workforce investment councils has provided a mechanism of planning and oversight, although the powers and scope of these councils vary from state to state. By far the most common approach has been that which some state officials describe as centrally guided, locally directed efforts, with states creating overall goals and local councils directing their implementation. What seems to be happening, in the fitful way typical of American federalism, is that the entire structure of state and local efforts is lurching in the direction of greater coordination.

The Checkered Role of the Federal Government

The problem of proliferating education and training programs, with inconsistent purposes and regulations, has been a problem of federal policy to some extent. In response, federal legislation has incorporated small measures to improve coordination, ranging from mandatory planning activities, to JTPA funds earmarked for coordination, to encouragement of state consolidation. In 1996, proposed federal legislation to combine federal funding for vocational education, adult education, and job training did not pass; the WIA that did pass, in August 1998, has maintained separate funding for job training and adult education, with vocational education funded in still other legislation.

Although it is still too early to know what the effects of WIA will be, it might—with one important exception—contribute to the development of coherent systems. It continues the state-local structure of workforce investment boards that many states have already adopted. It encourages states to submit unified plans for up to fourteen federal programs to ensure their coordination. It also strengthens the role of one-stop centers, principally by establishing them as the access point for employment-related training and other services. In addition, the act provides further incentives to improve the quality of programs, particularly by requiring indicators of performance and establishing incentive grants starting in the year 2000 to states with above-average performance. Because the low quality and unresponsiveness of programs is one factor preventing their coordination with others—for example, in the reluctance of many providers to refer to adult education— the improvement of quality should encourage programs to work with one another.

However, WIA places new emphasis on individual training accounts, in which participants choose among providers, and it deemphasizes the provision of training through contracts with specific providers. But when individuals rather than program administrators are the principal decision makers, they may or may not decide to enroll in programs that are well coordinated with others. Consumer choice may be influenced by many factors (like proximity and convenience) other than the quality of programs, the comprehensiveness of services, and links to other providers. The development of coherent systems of workforce development programs may therefore be undermined by greater reliance on this voucher-like approach. The WIA is therefore somewhat ambiguous in its influences, and it will no doubt take some time for its effects to become known.

The Potential Role of Postsecondary Vocational Education

In the uneven development of workforce development systems, vocational education—and community college and some area vocational centers in particular—have played various roles. Even in the absence of active state policy, community colleges have often served as contractors to job training and welfare programs, providing assessment, remedial education, and vocational programs of varying length. In some communities, the community college has been the only provider of virtually all education and training services, and in a few states community colleges have administered JTPA, adult education, and economic development programs. In states like North Carolina, Oregon, and Oklahoma, where community colleges have strong reputations and well-connected vocational programs, they have become the linchpins of state systems; they provide a variety of education and training, as well as economic development activities, and they are often central to the planning of local workforce investment councils. In some states, community colleges are actively participating in efforts to develop programs for welfare recipients under the new welfare legislation. However, in states where community colleges are perceived as weak, academically oriented, or inflexible in their schedules, or where they have not participated in early discussions, they are often left out of state coordination efforts altogether. When this occurs, the continued separation of education from training means that the majority of funding for workforce development efforts remains outside state reforms (Grubb and others, 1999).

But the more serious problem of the continuing division between education and workforce development is that in a coherent system, programs could learn from one another and provide more comprehensive and effective services. For example, many training and welfare-to-work programs are forced to provide remedial education, usually in poorly designed programs with low-quality teaching based on "skills and drills." Efforts in some community colleges to teach remedial education in coherent developmental studies departments, or in learning communities where basic skills are taught in the context of vocational courses, provide more effective approaches. Similarly, the efforts to integrate academic and vocational education, developed in high schools and community colleges with the support of federal funds, provide more powerful ways of teaching the multiple competencies called for by many employers and commissions, including SCANS. These practices could be adopted in many job training programs as well. A few colleges have developed strong links between school-based and work-based learning, through cooperative education, school-to-work programs, and school-based enterprises, providing yet another model for others to follow. And the best community colleges pride themselves on being teaching institutions. They use a variety of institutional policies to strengthen the quality of teaching, a dimension that is almost completely missing from job training, welfare-related, and adult education programs (Grubb and Associates, 1999).

Conversely, education providers have much to learn from job training. Community colleges often have lax placement efforts and weak connections with local employers. They could learn from job training programs that have placed greater emphasis on targeting efforts on the most promising employment and finding jobs as well as preparing their clients for them. Education providers could also learn from job training and adult education about flexible and unconventional scheduling, because they are often charged as being wedded to rigid academic calendars.

Furthermore, some outcomes are possible only within an integrated system. The small benefits of short-term job training programs are due in part to the low intensity of services (most last only ten to fifteen weeks) and the provision of a limited range of services to individuals with multiple barriers to employment. In the absence of substantial funding increases, these problems cannot be resolved without linking existing programs together. For example, programs of increasing complexity could be connected in ladders of opportunity, with an individual attending one or two short job training programs and then, as time and employment demands permit, transferring into related certificate and associate degree programs in community colleges or technical institutes. This vision specifies a particularly crucial role for community colleges and technical institutes as the bridges between short-term remedial and training programs and the mainstream educational system. The cooperation among different programs (including those providing noneducational services like child care and health care) is a solution to the need for more comprehensive services. These reforms, which rely on existing institutions rather than creating new ones, require that all providers be better integrated.

What remains to be seen is whether this vision of coherent workforce development systems that cover both education and training will be implemented in the coming years. Certainly, the most active states are now moving in this direction, with some help, however checkered, from federal policy. In many others, the standard complaints about the existing system—about duplication and waste, ineffectiveness and murkiness—have created pressures in the same direction. Historically, Americans have been fond of system building, evidently because the benefits outweigh the costs of uniformity and potential rigidity. In such a world, it makes no sense for any programs, including vocational education, to continue working in lonely isolation.

References

Grubb, W. N. *Learning to Work: The Case for Reintegrating Job Training and Education.* New York: Russell Sage Foundation, 1996.

Grubb, W. N., Brown, C., Kaufman, P., and Lederer, J. *Innovation Versus Turf: Coordination Between Vocational Education and Job Training Partnership Act Programs.* Berkeley: National Center for Research in Vocational Education, University of California at Berkeley, Apr. 1989.

Grubb, W. N., and Kalman, J. "Relearning to Earn: The Role of Remediation in Vocational Education and Job Training." *American Journal of Education,* 1994, 103, 54–93.

Grubb, W. N., and McDonnell, L. "Combating Program Fragmentation: Local Systems of Vocational Education and Job Training." *Journal of Policy Analysis and Management,* 1996, 15, 252–270.

Grubb, W. N., and Associates. *Honored But Invisible: An Inside Look at Teaching in Community Colleges.* New York: Routledge, 1999.

Grubb, W. N., and others. *Toward Order from Chaos: State Efforts to Reform Workforce Development "Systems."* Berkeley: National Center for Research in Vocational Education, University of California at Berkeley, 1999.

Hollinger, D., and Harvey, J. "Coordinating Vocational Education and Federal Job-Training Programs." In L. Muraskin, D. Hollinger, and J. Harvey (eds.), *Funding and Administrative Issues.* Washington D.C.: Office of Educational Research and Improvement, U.S. Department of Education, July 1994.

National Commission on Education and the Economy. *American's Choice: High Skills or Low Wages!* Rochester, N.Y.: National Commission on Education and the Economy, 1990.

Secretary's Commission on Achieving Necessary Skills. *What Work Requires of Schools: A SCANS Report for America 2000.* Washington, D.C.: U.S. Department of Labor, June 1991.

W. NORTON GRUBB *is professor and David Gardner Chair in Higher Education at the School of Education, University of California at Berkeley.*

Community colleges are forging a wide range of partnerships and collaborations with other community interests and resources to create a variety of vocational education opportunities. Examples are provided to illustrate new directions and innovative practices. Limitations of collaborations are also discussed.

Community Colleges and Their Communities: Collaboration for Workforce Development

Margaret Terry Orr

Collaborating with various community sectors is becoming an integral part of how community colleges undertake workforce development, particularly for the new vocationalism. In recent years, community colleges increasingly have forged formal and informal relationships with employers, labor, public schools, universities, community agencies, and other entities to create new or improved vocational programs and services and promote broader strategic planning for workforce development. This chapter explores the nature of, incentives for, and challenges of wide-ranging community college partnerships and collaborations.

The new vocationalism reflects a growing emphasis on vocational-technical education for growth industries of the new economy, incorporating academic outcomes (W. N. Grubb, personal communication, Feb. 1, 2001); a market-driven responsiveness to ever-changing business and industry skill needs (Zeiss, 1999–2000); and an emphasis on lifelong learning that is focused on skill rather than degree acquisition. According to Bragg (1997), the new vocationalism is more holistic in its educational approach than traditional vocational education is by combining academic and vocational-technical skill development needed for the new economy and improving articulation across educational levels. To develop their capacity for such approaches, community colleges are using collaborative arrangements with other educational entities and the business and government sectors of their communities. These entities and sectors seek out community colleges as part of their strategic workforce development plans by forging new joint, interrelated efforts.

The push for increased community college collaboration comes from all sectors: community colleges, businesses, community organizations, and government agencies. In 2000, in a report entitled *The Knowledge Net,* the American Association of Community Colleges (AACC) argued that community colleges should increase their collaborations with business, industry, and other educational entities as a primary strategy to develop a higher-quality, better-prepared workforce. AACC also argued that community colleges should gain resources and expertise from business partners and reduce potential duplication through collaboration with educational partners.

Zeiss (1999–2000) underscored the need for community colleges to redesign their programs and services in closer collaboration with their communities, particularly business and industry. First, he argued, there is a great need for better-skilled workers: "Every community is crying out for more skilled and productive workers, and businesses and trade associations are scrambling to develop dependable sources for providing new workers. Employers are equally concerned about keeping existing workers trained with the skills needed to be more productive" (p. 48). Second, he pointed out, business and industry are looking for certified occupational and workplace skills, not degrees. Zeiss urges community colleges to recognize this trend and respond proactively. Third, he explained that if community colleges are not more responsive in providing a more market-driven, community-integrated role, they will be ignored as business and industry look for and develop more relevant training and preparation services. His solution is for community colleges to transform themselves into "a consumer-driven, open learning delivery system" (p. 48) that is more integrated with other educational levels and business and industry, through strategic planning, collaborations, and redesigned programs and services.

The business community also promotes community college collaboration as strategic workforce development. Businesses, including Texas Instruments, have turned to community colleges to develop industry-specified vocational programs. Based on his experience with such partnerships, Swindle (1999) argued that partnerships of business and industry with community colleges are necessary to improve the workforce through more advanced academic and technical skill development, thereby improving competition in the global economy.

Finally, the federal and state governments now often include a provision encouraging or even requiring collaboration in new workforce development initiatives. For example, community college partnerships with school districts were key elements of the Tech Prep Education Act of 1990 and 1998. Building a seamless technical education delivery system from secondary through postsecondary education to employment is also a priority in the recently reauthorized Carl D. Perkins Vocational and Applied Technology Education Act of 1998. Moreover, the School-to-Work Opportunities Act (STWOA) of 1994 encouraged regional collaborations involving business, public education, and postsecondary education, including community colleges. In addition, individual states have launched their own workforce development initiatives that incorporate community college collaboration with business and education (Illinois Community College Board, 1997).

Forging a seamless transition across several educational levels reflects a re-visioning of educational systems from elementary education through college using improved articulation and transitions and more integrated programs and services. According to the AACC (2000), community colleges can play a central role in such a transformation through collaborative relationships, implying that these colleges could serve a wide range of educational needs within the context of the new vocationalism.

The goal for such collaborative efforts, according to AACC (2000), is for community colleges to prepare people by guiding "the development of technologically competent people who will be sensitive to the impact of their actions in the workplace, the community, and the world. They must produce people with occupational skills who also can think critically, solve problems, work and live ethically, and contribute to a democracy" (p. 35).

About Collaboration

Collaborations became popular in business, government, and communities during the 1980s (Gray, 1985) and continue to proliferate (Barney and Hesterley, 1996). Collaborations (and partnerships, as they are often classified) refer to some form of strategic joint relationship between two or more organizational entities. These relationships can be distinguished on the basis of on the purposes of the relationship and the products or services that are produced and how formalized they are, and whether a separate entity manages the relationship.

According to Barney and Hesterley (1996), organizations primarily enter into strategic alliances in order to "exploit resource complementarity" (p. 138) and generate economic value greater than their individual values. Among the motives for strategic alliance are opportunities for economies of scale, low-cost entry into new markets or segments, managing strategic uncertainty, and managing costs and sharing risks. Such motives are a common basis for community colleges' collaborations with business and industry and other educational entities in order to forecast workforce development needs, develop new training opportunities, identify new student markets, and create training and preparation specializations.

Collaborations are also increasingly used by organizations as a problem-solving strategy, particularly to address problems that the organization cannot solve alone (Gray, 1985). Especially challenging problems for bureaucratic organizations like public schools and two- and four-year colleges are those that are based on "decisions taken by other organizations" (Gray, 1985, p. 914), such as federal and state policy directives. According to Gray, organizations often fail to address such problems effectively because they frame them from their own perspective rather than a broader, more encompassing one. With a more interdependent (or ecological) perspective formed through collaborative interorganizational efforts, organizations could "coordinate their activities and manage the problem collectively rather than individually" (p. 916).

Problem-solving-focused collaboration underscores some of the arguments for how community colleges should align with business, industry, and other educational entities to address local workforce preparation priorities and other educational needs. According to Hockaday and Puyear (2000), community colleges can no longer address local educational and workforce development priorities in isolation. Instead, they must work with a wide variety of partners from all sectors of their local communities in order to develop more responsive and relevant programs, particularly for the new vocationalism.

Types of Collaboration

These reasons for strategic alliances are a useful framework for understanding community colleges and their collaborative relationships. Community colleges have several key resources, which can be the basis for collaborative relationships or part of more complex forms of cross-sector collaboration. These resources include the community college's mechanisms and processes for packaging and delivering course work and training, career guidance and counseling services, expertise in academic skill assessment and developmental course work, traditional classroom and high-tech training facilities, and overall flexibility and adaptability to expand and revamp programs and services.

The primary resources that community colleges gain through strategic alliances are improved educational pathways into their programs and services and in transferring students to four-year college programs; better access to student markets, particularly for those who can persist in college-level work; and improved forecasting of changing workforce development needs that have implications for programs, curriculum, and student recruitment. Using these forms of collaborations and others commonly found in the research literature (Hockaday and Puyear, 2000; Orr, 1999), Table 4.1 summarizes common purposes for community college collaborations for three primary partners: secondary schools, four-year colleges, and business and industry.

Several examples have been drawn from the literature to illustrate the potential for and emerging nature of the complex collaborations forged by community colleges as part of the new vocationalism. These examples show the breadth, diversity, and complexity of collaborations between community colleges and other sectors for the purposes listed in Table 4.1.

First, community colleges are forming many collaborations with secondary schools and K–12 systems, often as part of local STWOA initiatives

Table 4.1. Types of Partnerships and Collaborations at Community Colleges by Sector

Sector	Types of Partnerships or Collaborations
Secondary schools	Dual-enrollment courses for advanced high school courses and early college-level courses Accelerated college credit accumulation for the transition from high school to college Professional development for public school teachers Academic and vocational-technical skill assessment College and career counseling and guidance
Postsecondary institutions, four-year colleges	Transfer programs Course and program articulation
Business and industry	Preservice workforce development Inservice workforce development and retraining, tailored to major employers in the region
Combined sectors	Articulated programs of study from high school through community colleges and four-year colleges, focused on skill training in targeted high-growth industries

or tech prep partnerships. One example of a large-scale career and college exploration and guidance partnership was undertaken by Pima Community College in Arizona. This community college developed several outreach programs, including the Summer Career Academy, to improve linkages with K–12 school systems and student transitions, particularly in preparing for careers (Merren, Hefty, and Soto, 1997). The community college worked with two counties' school-to-work partnerships and local business and industry, using federal grant funding, to create a three-credit community college course with field trips, guest speakers, and other supporting activities. To provide students with career exploration opportunities among fifteen occupational areas, twenty-one summer academies were offered to 403 juniors and seniors from thirty-six high schools and alternative schools.

High schools and community colleges also offer concurrent course enrollment, at state encouragement, to enable high school students to take advanced courses and earn college credit. This measure enriches the local high school curriculum and broadens the student base for community colleges (Palmer, 2000). Several states also encourage dual-credit college courses, taught by community college faculty at high schools, enabling high school students to earn both high school and college credit (Andrews, 2000).

Furthermore, business and industry increasingly turn to community colleges to provide new types of vocational-technical training and form new organizational structures to support these efforts. For example, the Gulf Coast Process Technology Alliance was formed as a regional technology-specific alliance in process technology. This alliance encompasses industry, community colleges, and local government to prepare a workforce in process technology (Raley, 2000). Such partnerships do not have to be local and may draw on a single source of community college expertise. For example, a partnership was formed among the Association of Rotational Molders, El Paso Community College, Texas, and the College of DuPage, Illinois, to develop a curriculum package for in-house training, community college customized training, and continuing-education programs for production technicians in the rotational molding process (El Paso Community College, College of DuPage, and Association of Rotational Molders, 1998).

Finally, some collaborations entail elaborate partnerships across all sectors as a regional workforce development effort. For example, Central Piedmont Community College developed the Workforce Development Continuum as one of four initiatives in a strategic plan for the Charlotte, North Carolina, region "to provide a continuous stream of qualified workers in all career fields" (Zeiss, 1999–2000, p. 48). Governmental, business, and educational leaders developed this strategic plan. The community college's initiative is designed as a "knowledge-supply chain for emerging, existing, entrepreneurial, and transitional workers" and a "pipeline of skilled and re-skilled workers in a collaborative effort with government, business and the community at large" (p. 49). The intent is to forge a "seamless education and training system from four-year-olds through graduate school with easily accessible and convenient skills upgrading component" (p. 49). The system will be based on standardizing education and vocational-technical competencies to meet market standards and as a basis for more relevant courses, certifications, and degree programs.

In summary, many community college collaborations involve three or four types of sectors and often multiple entities from within each sector, such as several business partners or several schools and school districts. The examples here are not necessarily unusual or exemplary, but demonstrate the scope of collaborative work that community colleges undertake to develop new markets and help address the educational and workforce development needs of their communities. Multifaceted alliances depend on interinstitutional relationships, which are quite complex and fraught with potential pitfalls. A closer look at interorganizational collaborations can provide useful insights and reveal challenges that community colleges face in their local collaborations.

Collaboration Structure

Collaborations are characterized by how much and in what ways the inter-relatedness of participating organizations is structured, including governance and use of resources. According to Gray (1985), the nexus of an interorganizational relationship is the set of interdependencies that link them. Most commonly, the structure of collaborative relationships among community colleges appears to be associated with the scope and intensity of shared efforts (Orr, 1999). That is, more complex relationships are more likely to require their own staffing and administrative structures.

The interdependence among collaborating institutions can range from information sharing, coordinating services, and sharing of services and resources, to joint planning and joint action, the most extensive (Langman and McLaughlin, 1993; Orr, 1999). Sharing community college guidance and resources with local high schools reflects the more limited forms of collaboration. In contrast, integrated, growth industry–based programs involving multiple high schools, a community college, and a four-year college reflect a much more elaborate form of interdependence in joint planning, coordinated action, and shared resources.

Collaborations, particularly the more complex and interdependent ones, require attention to their own organizational attributes and potential pitfalls to be effective. First, collaborations have three general developmental phases: problem setting, in which stakeholders determine the nature and substance of their interdependence and believe that interdependence will produce positive outcomes; direction setting, whereby common values and goals are established to which the collaborating organizations can subscribe; and structuring, to support and sustain their collective efforts (Gray, 1985). All three phases are influenced by the degree to which the partnering agencies can develop a shared understanding of the problems, how much they perceive themselves to be interdependent, how power is dispersed and shared among the stakeholders, and the efficacy of the structures established to address shared goals. Finally, to be successful, collaborations need a process for monitoring change within and external to their shared efforts.

Second, collaborative relationships are influenced by many factors, particularly how much the partnering agencies or organizations perceive the value of the resource complementarity, their institutional context (Barney and Hesterley, 1996), the trust among partners (Clegg and Hardy, 1996), and whether collaborations are voluntary (Gray, 1985). Mandated collaboration may be less successful because collaborating organizations fail to address their interdependence and balance of power. They often give insufficient attention to each phase of development.

Third, several attributes of collaborating organizations can affect collaborative relationships and enable organizations to override existing institutional boundaries to forge new endeavors (Langman and McLaughlin, 1993). Five of these attributes and how they can facilitate or hinder community college collaborations follow:

• *Structures and routines,* which define the manner in which day-to-day operations are carried out. For example, schools and community colleges typically have differing schedules, curricula, and courses of study, which challenge course articulation and dual-enrollment efforts.

• *Organizational capacity,* which consists of resources, including money, staffing, facilities, and expertise, that enable the collaborations. For example, community colleges, public schools, and business and industry would all contribute different resources and expertise to a collaboratively organized program of study. Although these resources can enable the collaboration, the disparities can be a source of tension in decision making and problem solving.

• *Organizational domains,* which refers to the "institutional fields in which an organization's service falls and in which it has developed expertise" (Langman and McLaughlin, 1993, p. 163) and includes the potential for turf conflict. Community colleges, public schools, four-year colleges, and business and industry may all define their service areas differently. Greater coherence in service boundaries can simplify coordination efforts. At the same time, however, the same educational institutions may find themselves in competition over the same students or as increased collaboration makes them more aware of and thus in competition for new markets and services.

• *Organizational belief system,* which reflects the expressed and unexpressed goals of each organization and how these goals are complementary or competing. Community colleges, public schools, four-year colleges, and business and industry may share common goals in a collaborative workforce development effort while having differing and even competing goals and objectives in their other work. Within the community college, faculty and staff share beliefs about how postsecondary education and training should be carried out for youth and adults. New approaches, forged through collaborative efforts, should take into account these internal organizational belief systems and engage faculty and staff productively.

• *Organizational power and legitimacy,* which encompasses each organization's broader sphere of political influence. Through collaborative efforts, community colleges, business and industry, public schools, and other entities can generate political influence through individual efforts or unique endeavors. This political influence can help with public local and state funding, as well as private funding and support.

These five attributes are both the basis for structuring collaboration among organizational entities and the source of dilemmas and conflict among partnering organizations. The effort needed to develop and sustain collaborations can be costly for the partnering institutions because of the time and commitment necessary. Other concerns include the potential of diminishing institutional uniqueness and the possibility of making client access and services more difficult because of the new layers of bureaucracy. As a result, collaborative partnerships can be less fruitful than their potential would suggest. For example, national evaluations of tech prep and STWOA, which commonly encouraged secondary schools to collaborate with community colleges, have revealed that partnering community colleges and secondary schools often have difficulty identifying program participants, defining curriculum elements, and sharing information (Bragg and others, 1997; Hershey, Silverberg, Owens, and Hulsey, 1998).

In addition, community colleges sometimes have to convince other potential partners they can contribute to workforce development, particularly as part of the new vocationalism. For example, Zeiss (1999–2000) observed that the community college where he served as president was not initially included in strategic planning efforts in forging a regional workforce development continuum. He "had to lobby hard to ensure that our college was considered a major factor in the community's strategic plan, 'Advantage Carolina'" (p. 48). Zeiss faulted community planners for not recognizing that most jobs would not require a baccalaureate degree and for overlooking the fact that the community college has a vast education and training infrastructure.

Finally, a commonly cited consequence of collaboration for community colleges is the loss of uniqueness. According to Hockaday and Puyear (2000), "The number and variety of partnerships in which community colleges participate will further blur mission boundaries" (p. 8). This mission blurring, both within the community college itself and in partnership with others, may make it more challenging for community colleges to set priorities and chart new directions, given their bounded resources and capacity.

Conclusion

The new vocationalism stresses complex collaborative relationships among educational sectors, business and industry, and other entities. Such relationships are needed to forecast education and training requirements effectively, develop flexible and adaptable skill-focused preparation, articulate course sequences, and integrate academic and vocational education. Community colleges can have a central role in these complex new collaborations, building on their expertise in advanced vocational-technical skill development, degree program design and delivery, and articulation capacity with both public secondary education and four-year colleges.

Such collaborations offer many benefits for community colleges in expanding their student markets, improving their strategic forecasting for workforce development programs and services, and integrating them more fully in their region's workforce development efforts. But the complexity of these collaborative relationships can make them cumbersome to negotiate and sustain. More attention to the structures that support common goals, purposes, and interdependence is needed. Even so, community colleges bring considerable expertise to managing the dynamics of collaboration because of their experiences with other interinstitutional efforts. Certainly, their organizational capacity for collaboration makes them well suited for a central role in the new vocationalism.

References

American Association of Community Colleges. *The Knowledge Net: Connecting Communities, Learners and Colleges.* Washington, D.C.: American Association of Community Colleges, 2000.

Andrews, H. A. "Lessons Learned from Current State and National Dual-Credit Programs." In J. C. Palmer (ed.), *How Community Colleges Can Create Productive Collaborations with Local Schools.* New Directions for Community Colleges, no. 111. San Francisco: Jossey-Bass, 2000.

Barney, J. B., and Hesterley, W. "Organizational Economics: Understanding the Relationship Between Organizations and Economic Analysis." In S. R. Clegg, C. Hardy, and W. R. Nord (eds.), *Handbook of Organization Studies.* Thousand Oaks, Calif.: Sage, 1996.

Bragg, D. D. "Grubb's Case for Compromise: Can 'Education Through Occupations' Be More?" *Journal of Vocational Education Research,* 1997, *22,* 115–122.

Bragg, D. D., and others. *Tech Prep/School to Work Partnerships: More Trends and Challenges.* Berkeley: National Center for Research in Vocational Education, University of California at Berkeley, Dec. 1997.

Clegg, S. R., and Hardy, S. "Representations." In S. R. Clegg, C. Hardy, and W. R. Nord (eds.), *Handbook of Organization Studies.* Thousand Oaks, Calif.: Sage, 1996.

El Paso Community College, College of DuPage, and the Association of Rotational Molders. *Rotational Molding Process Technician. Instructional Program Package.* El Paso, Tex.: El Paso Community College, College of DuPage, and the Association of Rotational Molders, 1998.

Gray, B. "Conditions Facilitating Interorganizational Collaboration." *Human Relations,* 1985, *38,* 911–936.

Hershey, A. M., Silverberg, M. K., Owens, T., and Hulsey, L. K. *Focus for the Future: The Final Report of the National Tech Prep Evaluation.* Princeton, N.J.: Mathematica Policy Research, 1998.

Hockaday, J., and Puyear, D. E. *Community College Leadership in the New Millennium.* Washington, D.C.: American Association of Community Colleges, 2000. [199.75.76.25/initiatives/newexpeditions/white_papers/leadershiphite.htm.]

Illinois Community College Board. *Report on Community College Industrial Production Technology Programs.* Springfield: Illinois Community College Board, 1997.

Langman, J., and McLaughlin, M. W. "Collaborate or Go It Alone? Tough Decisions for Youth Policy." In S. B. Heathand and M. W. McLaughlin (eds.), *Identity and Inner-City Youth.* New York: Teachers College Press, 1993.

Merren, J., Hefty, D., and Soto, J. "School to College Linkage—New Models That Work." Paper presented at the annual meeting of the National Council for Occupational Education, San Antonio, Tex., Oct. 1997.

Orr, M. T. *Community College and Secondary School Collaboration on Workforce Development and Educational Reform: A Close Look at Four Community Colleges.* New York: Community College Research Center, Teachers College, May 1999.

Palmer, J. C. "Demographics, State Education Reform Policies, and the Enduring Community College Role as an Extension of the Schools." In J. C. Palmer (ed.), *How Community Colleges Can Create Productive Collaborations with Local Schools*. New Directions for Community Colleges, no. 111. San Francisco: Jossey-Bass, 2000.

Raley, B. "The International Alliance for Process Technology: A Partnership for America's Future." *Community College Journal of Research and Practice*, 2000, *24*, 37–46.

Swindle, J. "Industry/Community Colleges: Allies in the War for Talent." *Community College Journal*, 1999, *69*, 16–19.

Zeiss, T. "Community/Workforce Development: A Mandate for Relevancy." *Community College Journal*, 1999–2000, *70*, 47–49.

MARGARET TERRY ORR *is associate professor of education in the Department of Organization and Leadership and senior research associate at the Community College Research Center at Teachers College, Columbia University, New York.*

5

This chapter focuses on the involvement of two-year colleges in tech prep within multiple workforce development partnerships particular to the unique geography of Texas. Results of a survey of Texas technical education administrators offer insights into how tech prep is perceived to have an impact on postsecondary technical programs.

Two-Year Colleges and Tech Prep Partnerships: A Texas Perspective

Carrie H. Brown

In Texas, state and federal legislation enacted during the 1980s and 1990s created multiple layers of workforce and economic development partnerships with overlapping goals and activities that had a direct impact on community colleges. Consequently, three additional partnerships joined the state's preexisting regional private industry councils associated with the Job Training Partnership Act and regional job services employer councils. In 1989, the first of these legislative acts codified vocational and technical planning committees voluntarily established in twenty-four regions, which included representatives of employers, training providers, public education, and postsecondary institutions. Known as quality workforce planning committees, these committees were charged with the coordination and enhancement of education and training in the region. Committee activities included analysis of regional labor market information and identification of targeted occupations for occupational and technical program improvement.

In 1991, a second layer of regional partnerships was added in response to the Tech Prep Education Act (1990) by the establishment of tech prep consortia coterminous with the state's workforce planning regions. This intentional arrangement served to integrate these consortia into the existing framework of partnerships and to help match tech prep program development with regional labor market demand. Shared advisory or executive committee membership facilitated the effective coordination of the first two

Support for the survey research described here came from federal Carl D. Perkins Tech Prep funds from the Texas Higher Education Coordinating Board to the Region 5 Education Service Center. Points of view or opinions expressed in this chapter may not necessarily represent official Texas Higher Education Coordinating Board position or policy.

partnerships. In fact, some of the quality workforce planning committees served as the advisory or executive committee for regional tech prep consortia, while others shared representatives. In 1999, state law codified these tech prep consortial structures.

This regional workforce development partnership structure was further complicated by the development of regional workforce development boards. Authorized by state legislation in 1995, they assumed several functions of quality workforce planning committees that were dissolved at about the same time.

Tech Prep Implementation in Texas

From the beginning, Texas took a comprehensive approach to the implementation of tech prep, attempting simultaneous statewide implementation to begin institutionalization of the initiative. Because of the size and geography of the state, this approach provided equal access to all schools and their students and allowed for targeted program development based on regional economic need within established statewide standards. Following a planning grant phase in 1991–1992, twenty-five regional consortia were awarded implementation grants, providing access to tech prep programs and processes to all fifty-seven two-year public colleges and the over 950 public independent school districts in the state with high schools (Nelson, 1994). All twenty-five consortia were funded for nearly ten or more years with an average annual consortium award of $300,000.

Texas consortia are composed of at least one community, technical, or two-year state college and a sufficient number of public independent school districts to represent collectively an adequate number of potential tech prep students for successful program implementation. The smallest consortium in the state consists of one community college and eight public independent school districts; the largest consists of ten community colleges and over eighty-five rural, suburban, and urban school districts (Brown, 2001a). On average, Texas tech prep consortia serve about thirty-eight independent school districts; 44 percent contain a single community college.

State-level policies also assist consortia in the development of tech prep programs and coordination of related activities. In 1993, the state's secondary and postsecondary education agencies adopted joint guidelines for state-level approval of program-level articulation agreements or six-year tech prep plans that include four years of high school and at least two years of postsecondary study. In that same year, processes were implemented to officially recognize associate degree programs with formal tech prep partnership agreements with secondary schools, and a new certificate credential, the enhanced skills certificate, was created to provide an avenue to recognize attainment of advanced skills (Texas Higher Education Coordinating Board, 1993). In addition, a statewide secondary tech prep student identifier was added to the state's public education information management system, and a code was created for high school transcripts to help colleges identify high school courses covered under course-level articulation agreements.

School-to-Work in Texas

Although preceded by the Tech Prep Education Act, the School-to-Work Opportunities Act (1994) was conceived as umbrella legislation designed to encompass the best reform strategies of tech prep career academies, youth apprenticeship, cooperative education, and other programs. Nationally, the development of local school-to-work systems is coordinated by school-to-work partnerships composed of educators and business, industry, and labor representatives, similar to tech prep. School-to-work legislation encourages development of a comprehensive system to address opportunity, learning, and wage gaps in student learners by linking the classroom with the workplace (Brustein and Mahler, 1994). The three basic components of school-to-work are intended to affect both secondary and postsecondary education and encompass school-based learning opportunities, work-based learning opportunities, and activities that ensure effective coordination of the two—so-called connecting activities.

Because of their strong community links and experiences with occupational and customized training, community colleges are positioned to play a major role in the development of school-to-work systems, functioning as leaders of partnerships composed of educators and their business, industry, and labor partners (Farmer and Key, 1997).

The complexity of school-to-work systems requires colleges to manage participation in multiple partnerships. By definition, the scope of a school-to-work system is broad, potentially encompassing all in-school and out-of-school educational and related work experiences from kindergarten through the university level and beyond. Development of such a system requires immense coordination and leveraging of funds from many different agencies and programs, including youth services, health and human services, and welfare reform initiatives. The melding of activities of these state and local social, governmental, and educational agencies makes it difficult to operationalize school-to-work as a distinct program, and even harder to assess the direct effects of school-to-work federal funds on educational programs and processes.

In Texas, school-to-work is defined as "a flexible, locally-selected group of activities focused upon a common theme of assisting interested young people in making a smooth transition from high school and college to work" (Impact Data Source and Texas Engineering Extension Service, 1999, p. 8). These diverse activities include the school-based, work-based, and connecting activities defined by federal law and coordinated by the state's twenty-seven regional partnerships formed under the direction of the Texas Workforce Commission. Of these, twelve currently share a single advisory board and staffs with tech prep consortia and serve as advisory committees to local workforce development boards. The remaining fifteen partnerships are either advisory or subcommittees of local workforce development boards. Community and technical college representatives serve on all twenty-seven school-to-career partnership committees. Despite multiple layers of workforce development and related partnerships, tech prep has maintained its status as the primary initiative for secondary and postsecondary technical program articulation.

Partnership Functions

Throughout this progression of regional partnership development, community and technical colleges in Texas have maintained a leadership role, performing multiple functions within. One of the functions of colleges is to serve as administrative agents for federal funds. Two-year colleges serve as the fiscal agents for twenty-three of the state's twenty-five tech prep consortia, and twelve of these colleges administer school-to-work federal funds as well. In this capacity, they serve as the employer of record and provide housing for the tech prep consortium and school-to-work partnership staff. College representatives also serve on consortium and partnership advisory or governing boards, and many serve as members of local workforce development boards. Depending on the regional partnership structure, some college representatives serve on all three partnership boards.

Community and technical colleges in Texas function as principal providers of education and training services for regional workforce and economic development, including tech prep associate degree programs, and they participate in various community outreach activities, including those sponsored by tech prep and school-to-work programs. Because tech prep and school-to-work partnerships coordinate activities and one or more of these partnerships are located on community college campuses, activities sponsored by these entities are readily associated with the college. These include college days, career fairs, job shadowing, internships for students and teachers, curriculum alignment and program articulation activities, and various staff development activities for high school and college teachers and counselors.

Impact of Tech Prep on Program Articulation and Content Integration

Perhaps the most comprehensive activity of tech prep consortia that has had a direct impact on community and technical college partners is the development of agreements that articulate technical course and program content. This is not surprising, considering the emphasis placed on the development of seamless educational pathways for students that span the secondary and postsecondary levels. Although this focus has produced a large number of articulation agreements among colleges and their secondary education partners across the nation, they most often focus on course-to-course content alignment rather than linking entire programs of study across educational levels (Hershey, Silverberg, Owens, and Hulsey, 1998). According to Pierce and Hull (1998), the first eight years of tech prep implementation have not significantly affected community colleges nationwide and consortia activities focused primarily on the development of articulation agreements built around existing college curricula.

Two principal levels of articulation link secondary and postsecondary instruction in Texas: course-to-course and program level. Course-to-course agreements compare secondary and postsecondary course content to determine equivalency, are developed between participating schools and colleges, and list criteria for the award of college credit for career and technology courses taken in high school. Program-level agreements require state-level approval and provide an outline of all courses required in the articulated secondary and postsecondary tech prep programs; hence, they are called six-year plans. These plans also indicate which technical courses within the plan articulate for postsecondary credit and courses eligible for dual credit through concurrent college enrollment.

Course-to-course agreements constitute key elements of articulated programs. Colleges in Texas report that in 1990, prior to tech prep legislation, they had entered into over 540 course-level articulation agreements, increasing by 1996 to over 8,900 individual agreements. This is an impressive proliferation of agreements, but it has become a paperwork burden for participating colleges, and it provides a confusing landscape for students and counselors because each agreement outlines different course content and expectations for awarding college credit.

In one articulation study in Texas, forty-six colleges reported eighteen different conditions that applied to the award of articulated college credit; only two of these conditions were cited by more than 34 percent of the respondents (Brown, 1998). As a result, Texas initiated a process for the statewide articulation of commonly articulated secondary career and technology courses that is expected to facilitate the matriculation of students to community colleges (Brown, 2000). Beginning in fall 2000, sixty-two of seventy-three community and technical college campuses across the state, representing almost 88 percent of the state's fifty-seven two-year colleges and college districts, voluntarily adopted the standard articulation agreement for courses eligible for statewide articulation.

When tech prep was first evaluated in 1993–1994, forty-four of fifty-seven two-year colleges in Texas had sought state approval for six-year tech prep programs (Jackson, Dial, and Strauss, 1994), and by 1999 all but one community college in Texas had obtained approval to offer these programs. These fifty-six colleges had approval for over 760 degree programs, over 830 certificate exit points, and almost 370 enhanced skills certificates. These approved degree programs represent tech prep program articulation agreements with over seven hundred public school districts in Texas (Brown, 2001a).

Although the integration of academic content into technical courses at the secondary level is widespread, integration of technical content into academic courses generally is not, though some progress has been reported. In fact, most postsecondary consortium members have not instituted these changes in their institutions, despite promotion of the concept through college-sponsored staff development activities (Hershey, Silverberg, Owens, and Hulsey, 1998). In their study of tech prep implementation, Bragg, Layton, and Hammons (1994), as well as Badway (1998), found little evidence of postsecondary curriculum reform, despite the extensive rationale for integrating vocational and academic education at the postsecondary level.

Perceptions of Two-Year Technical Education Administrators

In January 2001, eighty-three technical education administrators in the state's fifty-seven two-year colleges and college systems were surveyed to determine their college's level of involvement in tech prep processes and their perception of the impact of tech prep on the college's technical programs (Brown, 2001b). Fifty-six college administrators responded, for a return rate of 67.5 percent, representing 82.5 percent of the state's colleges and twenty-one tech prep consortia. Results indicate that Texas colleges in general are actively engaged in tech prep processes, yet 67.0 percent indicated that exclusive of tech prep, the school-to-work initiative had little or no impact on their college.

Three primary areas were covered by the survey: level of participation in tech prep activities, methods used to encourage and record student participation in postsecondary tech prep programs, and perceived impact of tech prep on college technical programs. Perception of the overall impact of tech prep on the college's technical programs, ranked significant, moderate, minimal, or none, was compared to responses to each of these three areas.

Level of Participation in Tech Prep Activities. This survey area provided a list of activities commonly associated with implementation of tech prep. Almost 68 percent of colleges responding to the survey indicated that one or more college representatives have served on the tech prep consortium's advisory board. About 95 percent also reported college participation in one or more additional tech prep activities, including hosting curriculum alignment and articulation meetings, faculty and counselor staff development activities, and high school student activities such as college days and career fairs.

Almost 68 percent of respondents indicated they had hosted course or program curriculum alignment meetings for their secondary partners. Although over three-fourths of Texas two-year colleges stated they participated in faculty and staff development activities and nearly 68 percent in counselor staff development activities, 46 percent responded that tech prep provided additional options for college faculty and staff development, suggesting that tech prep staff development focuses primarily on the needs of secondary school teachers. Other than fiscal or advisory service, almost 68 percent of colleges indicated participation in three or more tech prep–related activities, and about 43 percent indicated participation in five activities.

Significantly, over 48 percent of colleges indicated that the overall impact of tech prep on their college's technical programs is significant (19.6 percent) or moderate (28.6 percent). Only four administrators, or about 7 percent of respondents, indicated no impact on their technical programs. Interestingly, of the nearly 45 percent of college administrators reporting minimal impact, over half are located in the two largest, multicollege tech prep consortia in the state.

Figure 5.1 illustrates responses to a survey question concerning level of participation in tech prep grouped according to the respondent's perception of the overall impact of tech prep on his or her college's technical programs. Of the twenty-seven college administrators reporting significant or moderate impact, about 52 percent served as the tech prep consortium's fiscal agent, and almost 93 percent served on the consortium's advisory board. In contrast, for the twenty-nine colleges reporting minimal to no effect, only 17 percent and 45 percent, respectively, served in these capacities.

The other five areas listed included hosting curriculum and program alignment meetings, participation in faculty and counselor staff development activities, and participation in student activities such as college days and career fairs. Of the colleges reporting significant or moderate impact, responses ranged from 67 percent (hosting tech prep alignment meetings) to 89 percent (participation in faculty staff development). Each area of response was higher by about 8 percentage points to 23 percentage points than colleges reporting minimal to no effect.

Methods to Encourage and Record Student Participation. A number of strategies have been employed by two-year colleges in Texas to identify tech prep students who are making the transition to postsecondary institutions, and this survey provided a list of nine items pertaining to student transition. Almost 88 percent of the respondents indicated they placed descriptions of tech prep in the college bulletin or catalog, about 66 percent used counseling or other staff to recruit high school tech prep students, and 63 percent included information on tech prep in college advising procedures. In addition, about 52 percent hired an articulation or tech prep coordinator (not including consortium staff), about 41 percent sent letters about tech prep and articulated credit to parents and students, and a fourth placed tech prep or other staff in a prominent location during registration.

Nevertheless, as of fall 2000, on average, fewer than half of the state's two-year colleges could accurately report continuing high school tech prep students on their campuses or report the number of articulated credits awarded the previous year (Texas Higher Education Coordinating Board,

Figure 5.1. Level of College Participation in Tech Prep and Perceived Impact on Technical Programs

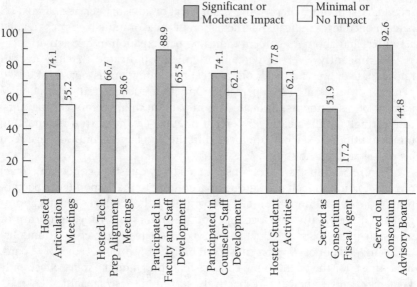

Source: Brown (2001b).

2000). Of survey respondents, just over 53 percent indicated they recorded the number of articulated credits awarded to students, 48 percent utilized a database of tech prep students on their campus, and less than one-third placed an indicator of high school tech prep participation on the college's admission or registration form.

Figure 5.2 shows responses to a survey question regarding student transition grouped according to respondents' perception of the overall impact of tech prep on college technical programs. Of colleges indicating significant or moderate impact, over 70 percent indicated that they hired an articulation coordinator, almost 78 percent used college counselors or other staff for recruiting, and 74 percent included tech prep in their advising process. Of respondents in this category, about 82 percent reported using three or more of the six active recruitment and matriculation strategies, about two-thirds used four or more, and over a third used five or more. Of the three remaining strategies, 48 percent reported that they used a database of entering tech prep students, 59 percent indicated they recorded articulated credit awarded, and 48 percent sent letters to students and parents about tech prep.

In contrast, for colleges indicating minimal or no impact, only about 35 percent indicated that they hired an articulation coordinator, and about 55 percent used college counselors or other staff for recruiting or included tech prep in their advising process. Of respondents in this category, only 52 percent reported using three or more of the six active recruitment and

Figure 5.2. Level of College Participation in Tech Prep Student Recruitment and Identification and Perceived Impact on Technical Programs

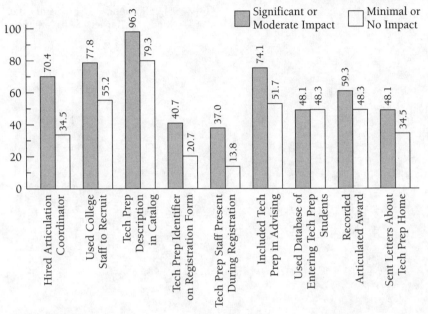

Source: Brown (2001b).

matriculation strategies, about one-fifth used four or more, and only 3 percent used five or more. Similar to moderate to significant impact groups, 48 percent reported that they used a database of entering tech prep students. However, of the minimal or no impact group, fewer indicated that they recorded articulated credit awarded, and only one-third sent letters to students and parents about tech prep.

Perceived Impact of Tech Prep on College Technical Programs. Although the ability of colleges to report tech prep students consistently statewide is less than adequate, colleges do report numerous benefits of participation in tech prep programs, in addition to enhancing articulation efforts and providing staff development activities. For example, about 36 percent of colleges responding reported an increase in technical program enrollment, 41 percent indicated supplemental funding, and about 36 percent reported improvements in postsecondary technical programs. Other benefits included increases in business, industry, and military partnerships (30 percent); development of new certificate options (21 percent); development of new degree programs or options (14 percent); and additional work-based learning experiences (18 percent). Few colleges report that the impact of tech prep on teaching methodologies (contextual and applied learning) in postsecondary classrooms is minimal (about 11 percent).

**Figure 5.3. Perceived Impact on College Technical Programs
by Area and Overall**

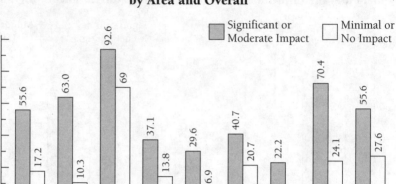

Figure 5.3 provides a comparison of individual areas affected by tech prep implementation grouped according to the respondents' perceptions of the overall impact of tech prep on technical programs. Of the colleges reporting significant or moderate impact, about 56 percent reported an increase in program enrollment, 63 percent reported program improvement, 93 percent reported enhanced articulation, and 70 percent reported increased opportunities for faculty and staff development. Responses to the remaining five areas ranged from 22 percent (changes in teaching methodology) to 56 percent (provided supplemental funding). Interestingly, almost 78 percent of those reporting significant to moderate impact reported two or more of the categories of increased enrollment, improved programs, and enhanced articulation, compared to only about 21 percent for those reporting minimal to no impact.

Of colleges reporting minimal to no effect, responses were significantly different. For example, only 17 percent reported an increase in program enrollment, 10 percent reported program improvement, and less than one-fourth reported increased faculty and staff development opportunities, although, not surprisingly, 69 percent reported enhanced articulation, the most common outcome of tech prep–related activities in Texas's two-year colleges. Responses to the remaining five areas ranged from 0 percent for changes in teaching methodology to 28 percent for supplemental funding.

Conclusion

By virtue of their mission, community and technical colleges play a pivotal role in the coordination of multiple levels of educational, economic, and community partnerships that link public education with business, industry, and labor. Tech prep and school-to-work initiatives exemplify these partnerships. According to a recent survey of technical education administrators in Texas, most two-year colleges actively participate in tech prep. In fact, nearly half of the public two-year colleges indicated that tech prep has had a moderate to significant impact on their college's technical programs, and not surprisingly, these colleges indicated more active involvement in tech prep–related activities. Colleges less actively involved tended to report fewer positive results and viewed tech prep as having minimal or no impact on college-level technical programs. Even so, two-thirds of respondents reported using three or more methods to identify and facilitate matriculation of high school tech prep students to two-year colleges.

Without question, community and technical colleges in Texas assume a leadership role in developing workforce and economic development in their communities, including implementing tech prep processes. Two-year colleges have hundreds of formal articulated plans with school districts that link to technical programs and are active in the statewide articulation initiative targeting technical courses. Undoubtedly, two-year colleges have benefited from participation in tech prep partnerships in numerous ways. Perhaps most important of all is improved communication between the colleges and their public education, business, industry, labor, and community partners.

References

Badway, N. "Extent, Quality and Access for Integrated Curriculum in Community Colleges." *Journal of Vocational Education Research*, 1998, *23*, 133–145.

Bragg, D. D., Layton, J. D., and Hammons, F. *Tech Prep Implementation in the United States: Promising Trends and Lingering Challenges.* Berkeley: National Center for Research in Vocational Education, University of California at Berkeley, 1994.

Brewer, J. A. *Integration of Academic and Occupational Education in Community/Technical Colleges.* Los Angeles: ERIC Clearinghouse for Community Colleges, 1999. (ED 425 786.)

Brown, C. H. *Evaluation Report Executive Summary: Statewide Implementation of Tech Prep in Texas.* Beaumont, Tex.: Region 5 Education Service Center, 1998.

Brown, C. H. *Statewide Articulation Guide and Standard Articulation Agreement.* Beaumont, Tex.: Region 5 Education Service Center, 2000.

Brown, C. H. *Closing the Gaps: How Tech Prep Programs Have Increased Participation and Success in Texas Schools: A Five-Year Study.* Beaumont, Tex.: Region 5 Education Service Center, 2001a.

Brown, C. H. *Statewide Evaluation of Tech Prep: Survey of Post-Secondary Technical Education Administrators.* Beaumont, Tex.: Region 5 Education Service Center, 2001b.

Brustein, M., and Mahler, M. *AVA Guide to the School-to-Work Opportunities Act.* Alexandria, Va.: American Vocational Association, 1994.

Farmer, E. I., and Key, C. B. "School-to-Work Systems and the Community College: Looking Ahead." In E. I. Farmer and C. B. Key (eds.), *The Role of Community Colleges in School-to-Work Systems.* New Directions for Community Colleges, no. 97. San Francisco: Jossey-Bass, 1997.

Grubb, W. N., and others. *Workforce, Economic, and Community Development: The Changing Landscape of the Entrepreneurial Community College.* Mission Viejo, Calif.: League for Innovation in the Community College, 1997.

Hershey, A. M., Silverberg, M. K., Owens, T., and Hulsey, L. K. *Focus for the Future: The Final Report of the National Tech Prep Evaluation.* Princeton, N.J.: Mathematica Policy Research, 1998.

Impact Data Source and Texas Engineering Extension Service. *Linking School-to-Careers with Economic Development: A Report of the Economic Impact of School-to-Careers in Texas.* College Station, Tex.: Impact Data Source and Texas Engineering Extension Service, 1999.

Jackson, R., Dial, M., and Strauss, R. *Evaluation of Tech Prep System Development and Implementation in Texas Public Schools and Institutions of Higher Education.* Houston: Decision Information Resources, 1994.

Nelson, C. H. "Tech Prep in Texas: An Implementation Strategy." *Community College Journal of Research and Practice,* 1994, *18,* 99–112.

Pierce, D., and Hull, D. "Changes for Community Colleges." In D. Hull and J. Grevelle (eds.), *Tech Prep the Next Generation.* Waco, Tex.: CORD Communications, 1998.

Texas Higher Education Coordinating Board. *Technical Education Program Guidelines.* Austin, Tex.: Texas Higher Education Coordinating Board, 1993.

Texas Higher Education Coordinating Board. *College Tech-Prep Enrollment Report—CBM 00T.* Austin, Tex.: Texas Higher Education Coordinating Board, 2000.

CARRIE H. BROWN *is a director of the Tech-Prep Statewide Technical Assistance Projects on Leadership and Evaluation at the Region 5 Education Service Center, Beaumont, Texas.*

6

The distinction between transfer and terminal education increasingly blurs as community college students once viewed as terminal begin to dominate the traditional transfer mission of the community college.

Blurring the Lines: Transforming Terminal Education to Transfer Education

Barbara K. Townsend

A new definition of community college transfer education is emerging. Initially defined as the general education component or first two years of a baccalaureate, transfer education is developing a de facto definition as those courses that transfer to a four-year college, regardless of the nature of the courses. Courses once designated as nontransfer or terminal education now often transfer to a four-year college. In some states, degrees once considered to be terminal or nontransfer degrees are being articulated with four-year degree programs at both the state and institutional levels. According to Debra Bragg in Chapter One of this volume, institutions that have a general education program with a specific connection to the applied degree or vocationally oriented courses are reflecting the paradigm of the new vocationalism. The viability of this paradigm is likely to be enhanced as more four-year colleges develop articulation agreements with community colleges for applied degree programs.

What accounts for this blurring of the concept of transfer education? In this chapter, I provide a historical perspective on this development, present current data, and discuss implications for two-year and four-year institutions.

A Historical Perspective

According to Koos (1970), an early advocate of terminal education, the junior college had three primary curricular functions: transfer education or "offering two years of work acceptable to colleges and universities," "the

provision of opportunities for 'rounding out general education,'" and terminal education or "preparation for occupations, the final training for which
would be given during junior-college years" (pp. 19–20). This last purpose
was also characterized as preparing people for the "semiprofessions" (p. 20),
differentiated "from *trades,* the training for which is concluded during the
conventional secondary-school period, and . . . from *professions,* adequate
preparation for which requires four or more years of training beyond the
high school" (p. 121). Semiprofessions during this time period were primarily in "commerce, engineering, and agriculture" (p. 135) and might
include such occupations as loan and stock brokers, draftsmen and survey-
ors, forest rangers, and florists. Nursing and teaching were also semiprofessions during this period. As Koos's definition of terminal education stated,
it was to be "the final training" (p. 19) for students preparing for a semi-
profession. In other words, these students were not expected to pursue further education—hence, the phrase *terminal education.*

Terminal students were not expected to transfer, thus potentially keeping academically unfit students out of the universities. By so clearly desig-
nating academic tracks for its students, the two-year college satisfied both
elitists who wanted to keep the universities selective and populists who
wanted further educational opportunities for Americans (Witt, Wattenbarger, Gollattscheck, and Suppiger, 1994).

Terminal education became an important function of the junior college, particularly during the Great Depression when people wanted education that would prepare them for available jobs. Seventy percent of junior
colleges offered one or more terminal programs by 1940 (Witt, Wattenbarger, Gollattscheck, and Suppiger, 1994). According to Eells's 1941 study
of junior college terminal education, 35 percent of students enrolled in
public junior colleges were in terminal education (Frye, 1992). However,
the junior college's dominant curricular mission continued to be transfer
education. As the junior college evolved into the community college during the 1950s and 1960s, terminal education, tied almost exclusively to the
vocational function, became increasingly important, stimulated partly by
federal monies for vocational education and partly by urgings of the American Association of Junior Colleges (Cohen and Brawer, 1996). By the
1980s, vocational education had become extremely important in two-year
colleges. Some of this growth was due to growing enrollments in for-profit
two-year colleges as well as in nonprofit technical institutes, part of some
states' two-year college systems.

As vocational education became more prominent in the community
college, its transfer or collegiate function came under increasing scrutiny.
Critics maintained that students who began their undergraduate education
at the community college in hopes of attaining a baccalaureate were less
likely to attain the degree than if they had begun at a four-year college (Brint
and Karabel, 1989). Also lamented has been the "decline in the percentage
of community college students who transfer to senior institutions," with

current estimates of transfer rates around 20 percent (Nora, 2000, p. 3). During the 1980s and 1990s, researchers and policymakers paid increasing attention to the movement of two-year students in transfer programs to the four-year college, the development of state-level articulation agreements, and ways to improve two-year colleges' transfer rates.

Most studies examining transfer rates defined transfer students as two-year students who were in transfer programs. However, there was some recognition that other kinds of transfer students existed. For example, Kintzer (1983) identified "the vocational transfer" student as "one who moves to a senior institution as a career/occupational degree candidate" (pp. 1–2) instead of as a liberal arts candidate. What Kintzer defined as the vocational transfer student is what was once described as the terminal education student—someone whose two-year college education focused on immediate entry into the workforce, not preparation for a baccalaureate. Kintzer perceived increasing attention to vocational transfers as more four-year colleges developed career-oriented undergraduate programs and worked with community colleges to develop joint degree programs.

Kintzer was not unique in his awareness of vocational transfers. Eells (1943) was one of the first to point out that some terminal program graduates transferred to senior colleges. He thought it important to record their success because it far exceeded others' expectations of graduates of these programs. Frye (1992), in his history of the public junior college from 1900 to 1940, asserted that many "students operated in terminal programs . . . as if they were preparatory [transfer] programs" (p. 115) and moved on to senior institutions. Looking at students in the 1980s, Carroll (1990) also included vocational transfers in a list of "clients" (p. 7) served by the community college's transfer mission.

Carroll (1990) also included as clients those individuals with a baccalaureate or higher who "transfer" to the two-year college. Labeled "post-baccalaureate reverse transfer students" by Townsend (1999), these students often attend the community college to retool in their current occupation or seek new skills to make a career change. Their presence in the community college is further demonstration of the blurring of terminal and transfer education.

Current Status of Transfer Among Vocational Education Students

The percentage of community college students currently enrolled in vocational education programs is high. A 1993 national study indicated that 93 percent of two-year colleges offered vocational education, and over 40 percent of two-year college students were enrolled in vocational education programs (Cohen and Brawer, 1996).

Although enrollment in transfer programs still exceeds that in vocational education programs, a higher percentage of associate degrees in applied fields are conferred annually than are degrees in the liberal arts. Of the more than 450,000 associate degrees conferred in 1996–1997, over 37 percent were in liberal or general studies and humanities. The rest were in vocationally oriented programs: health professions and related services with almost 77,000 degrees, business management and administrative services with almost 72,000 degrees, engineering-related technologies with over 20,000 degrees, and protective services with over 17,000 (Phillippe, 2000). Depending on how a state designates its associate degrees, applied degrees conferred include the following: the associate of applied science (A.A.S.), the associate of applied arts (A.A.A.), the associate of science (A.S.), the associate of specialized business (A.S.B.), and the associate in specialized technology (A.S.T.)(Bender, 1991).

Several researchers have noted that nationally, students with the A.A.S. degree are transferring in equal or even greater numbers than students with the traditional transfer degrees (Bernstein, 1986; Cohen and Brawer, 1996; Cohen and Ignash, 1994; Prager, 1988). There is clear evidence that many students in vocational education programs intend to transfer to a four-year college or university. Data from the 1995–1996 Beginning Postsecondary Students Longitudinal Study reveal that almost 32 percent of students in associate degree programs with majors in applied fields enrolled with intent to transfer to a four-year institution (Berkner, Horn, and Clune, 2000). This percentage reflects an increase of several points from the percentage found by Palmer (1987) in his national study of students in vocational programs. When he surveyed over seventy-five hundred students in ninety-five randomly selected two-year colleges, he found that 26 percent of the vocational students planned to transfer to a four-year college.

State studies that examine the transfer of vocational students also provide some evidence of their intentions, as well as their transfer behavior. Shearon, Brownlee, and Johnson (1990) studied North Carolina's community college students and found that almost half the students claimed they intended to transfer to a four-year college, although less than 20 percent were in transfer programs. Fredrickson (1998) also examined community college students in North Carolina after they had transferred in fall 1993 to a school in the University of North Carolina system. She found that 70 percent were from transfer programs and 30 percent from technical programs.

Implications for Research and Practice

Given the phenomenon of vocational education or terminal students transferring to four-year colleges, there are several implications for research and practice in both the two-year and four-year college sectors. These include the need to include students who transfer with an applied degree in any study of transfer rates that use degree completion as a variable. Typically, applied degree students are not included in transfer studies. For example, a recent statewide transfer study in Oregon (Oregon University System and

Oregon Department of Community Colleges and Workforce Development, 2000), in determining how many students transferred with a degree, considered only the A.A. or Oregon transfer degree. Statewide studies should also examine the educational background of two-year college transfers and compare the rate of transfer and baccalaureate-degree completion of students who transfer with the traditional transfer degree versus those who transfer with an applied degree.

Because the majority of community college students who transfer to a senior institution do so before receiving an associate degree (Coley, 2000), studies should also examine the extent to which vocational education courses transfer. Striplin (2000) conducted such a study when she examined the transferability of non–liberal arts courses offered by twenty-six California community colleges. She found that institutions in the California State University (CSU) system were far more likely to accept non–liberal arts courses than were University of California (UC) schools. Specifically, "in 1998, 72.6% of the non-liberal-arts courses transferred to the CSU System and 26.7% transferred to the UC System from California's community colleges" (p. 76).

Implications for practice include increasing transferable general education courses in terminal programs, possibly upgrading some technical college faculty's educational credentials, developing more interinstitutional articulation of vocational education courses and programs, and considering state-level articulation of all two-year college degrees and some applied programs.

General Education at the Two-Year College. Increasingly, state higher education systems, professional associations, and regional accrediting bodies are recommending or even mandating that applied programs contain a general education component. For example, the National Council for Occupation Education has recommended that this component be at least 25 percent of A.A.S. degree programs (Nolte, 1991). Illinois has endorsed this plan by mandating that students in A.A.S. programs receive fifteen hours of transfer-level general education courses. When requirements like this are made, the educational credentials of some two-year faculty will need to be upgraded.

Educational Credentials of Technical College Faculty. To comply with regional accrediting bodies' requirements, faculty who are teaching transfer-level general education courses need to have at least a master's degree, with eighteen or more graduate hours in their teaching field. Therefore, the educational credentials of faculty teaching general education courses at technical colleges often need to be upgraded (Findlen, 1997–1998). Increasing two-year college faculty credentials will enhance the credibility of two-year college courses when four-year and two-year college faculty work together to develop institutional programmatic and course articulation agreements.

Articulation of Vocational Courses and Programs. Individual four-year colleges and universities that enroll significant numbers of two-year college transfer students have well-developed articulation agreements with community colleges in their state. Typically, these agreements cover the A.A. degree (the transfer degree) and general education courses. Some institutions also have programmatic agreements that cover applied degrees and courses. Individual two- and four-year colleges may also articulate an A.A.S. degree with a bachelor's degree created for this purpose. For example, Northern Arizona University and Arizona State University have developed baccalaureate of applied science degrees that assume a student will transfer in an A.A.S. degree program.

Senior institutions are far less likely to have articulation agreements with technical colleges, let alone proprietary colleges, because of restrictive policies imposed by a state's major public university (Findlen, 1997–1998). For example, rather than having a system-level articulation agreement, the University of Wisconsin System (UWS) policy requires that each technical college in the Wisconsin Technical College System and each university in the UWS negotiate a program-to-program articulation agreement. Thus, a transfer student may receive credit at one UWS institution for vocational education courses but not at another (Findlen, 1997–1998).

A few high schools, two-year colleges, and four-year colleges have collaborated to develop 2+2+2 agreements. In these agreements, a vocational program links the last two years of high school with two years at a community college, resulting in an A.A.S., with two years at a senior institution, resulting in a baccalaureate. These 2+2+2 agreements are "very attractive in theory" but "exceedingly difficult to negotiate, partly because of ingrained skepticism that university faculty have for high school and even community college vocational education" (Bers, 1994, p. 255). Still, referencing actual results, Carrie H. Brown showed in Chapter Five of this volume that positive results are evident for tech prep programs in Texas when they are built on a solid curricular foundation.

Systemwide Degree and Applied Programs Articulation. While individual institutions can negotiate articulation agreements about A.A.S. and other applied programs as well as vocational education courses, it is helpful if the state has a policy that facilitates such transfer. Only one state, Maryland, has developed a state-level articulation agreement for an A.A.S. degree, and it is only for articulation with the B.S. in technology (Townsend and Ignash, 2000).

A few states have articulated specific applied programs. Arizona's state-level agreement includes a business program, as does Nevada. North Dakota has transfer agreements regarding nursing programs and construction and industrial technologies (Ignash and Townsend, 2000). Missouri is currently examining how its two-year college teacher education programs articulate with four-year college programs, with the goal being a seamless articulation that will lead to more teachers in the state (Missouri Coordinating Board of Higher Education, 2000).

These states' efforts need to be replicated by other states. It is time for policymakers to acknowledge that vocational education occurs in both two-year and four-year colleges and develop agreements that facilitate two-year college transfers in completing a baccalaureate degree in an applied major. The agreements should also address the transfer of non–liberal arts courses. Many states have developed state-level articulation agreements that include the transfer of general education credits, but few states have addressed the transfer of non–liberal arts courses.

The National Center for Research in Vocational Education has developed a taxonomy of academic and vocational courses for less-than-four-year postsecondary institutions. Drawing from this taxonomy, the Center for the Study of Community Colleges created a new one to indicate which courses were non–liberal arts courses at community colleges. Courses so designated fell into the following areas: agriculture, business and office, marketing and distribution, health, home economics, technical education, engineering technologies, trade and industry, personal skills and avocational courses, education, and other (Cohen and Ignash, 1994). Clearly, almost all four-year colleges and universities offer courses and programs in some or all of these areas. Thus, much of what is classified as vocational education takes place in four-year colleges as well as in two-year colleges. Only the level of the course work is different (at least in theory).

As evidence, recall Frederickson's study of North Carolina's transfer students (1998). She found that 53 percent of the students majored in ten university fields: nursing, elementary education, business management and administration, general psychology, criminal justice, accounting, general biology, engineering technologies, English, and political science and government. Nursing, elementary education, business management and administration, criminal justice, accounting, and engineering technologies are clearly vocational education programs found in two-year colleges.

Conclusion

Students have always attended the two-year college for their own purposes, which frequently run counter to the purposes intended by its founders and some current proponents (Frye, 1992; Oregon University System, 2000). Although state systems and individual colleges classify academic programs as transfer or nontransfer and assume students will behave accordingly once they complete the program, many students behave as though these classifications or tracks do not exist. Similarly, most state-level articulation agreements seem predicated on the assumption that two-year students intending to transfer to a four-year college will pursue an associate degree in the liberal arts. Consequently, few states have paid attention to the articulation of what are traditionally considered nontransfer degrees. Policymakers also seem unaware of how many four-year colleges and universities have developed degree programs for what were once classified as semiprofessions. With most senior institutions also in the business of providing vocational education or education for the semiprofessions, developing articulation agreements that facilitate the transfer of two-year-college vocational education courses and degrees into the equivalent senior programs seems logical.

References

Berkner, L., Horn, L., and Clune, M. *Descriptive Summary of 1995–96 Beginning Postsecondary Students: Three Years Later, with an Essay on Students Who Started at Less-Than-4-Year Institutions.* Washington, D.C.: National Center for Education Statistics, 2000.

Bender, L. "Applied Associate Degree Transfer Phenomenon: Proprietaries and Publics." *Community College Review,* 1991, *19,* 22–28.

Bernstein, A. "The Devaluation of Transfer: Current Explanations and Possible Causes." In L. S. Zwerling (ed.), *The Community College and Its Critics.* New Directions for Community Colleges, no. 54. San Francisco: Jossey-Bass, 1986.

Bers, T. "Articulation and Transfer." In A. Cohen, F. Brawer, and Associates, *Managing Community Colleges.* San Francisco: Jossey-Bass, 1994.

Brint, S., and Karabel, J. *The Diverted Dream: Community Colleges and the Promise of Educational Opportunity in America, 1900–1985.* New York: Oxford University Press, 1989.

Carroll, S. C. "The Transfer Mission." In D. Doucette and B. Hughes (eds.), *Assessing Institutional Effectiveness in Community Colleges.* Laguna Hills, Calif.: League for Innovation in Community Colleges, 1990.

Cohen, A., and Brawer, F. *The American Community College.* (3rd ed.) San Francisco: Jossey-Bass, 1996.

Cohen, A., and Ignash, J. M. "An Overview of the Total Credit Curriculum." In A. M. Cohen (ed.), *Relating Curriculum and Transfer.* New Directions for Community Colleges, no. 86. San Francisco: Jossey-Bass, 1994.

Coley, R. J. *The American Community College Turns 100: A Look at Its Students, Programs, and Prospects.* Princeton, N.J.: Educational Testing Service, 2000.

Eells, W. "Success of Transferring Graduates of Junior College Terminal Curricula." *Journal of American Association of Collegiate Registrars,* July 1943, pp. 372–398.

Findlen, G. L. "Technical Colleges and College Transfer—One More Time." *ATEA Journal,* Dec. 1997–Jan. 1998.

Fredrickson, J. "Today's Transfer Students: Who Are They?" *Community College Review,* 1998, *26,* 43–54.

Frye, J. *The Vision of the Public Junior College, 1900–1940.* Westport, Conn.: Greenwood Press, 1992.

Ignash, J. M., and Townsend, B. K. "Statewide Transfer and Articulation Policies: Current Practices and Emerging Issues." In B. K. Townsend and S. Twombly (eds.), *Community Colleges: Policy in the Future Context.* Norwood, N.J.: Ablex, 2000.

Kintzer, F. *The Multidimensional Problem of Articulation and Transfer.* Los Angeles: ERIC Clearinghouse for Community Colleges, 1983. (ED 288 577.) [http://www.ed.gov/databases/ERIC_Digests/ed288577.html.]

Koos, L. V. *The Junior-College Movement.* Westport, Conn.: Greenwood Press, 1970. (Originally published 1925.)

Missouri Coordinating Board of Higher Education Committee on Transfer and Articulation. "Charge to Teacher Education Articulation Advisory Committee." Columbia: Missouri Coordinating Board of Higher Education Committee on Transfer and Articulation, Dec. 7, 2000.

Nolte, W. H. "Guaranteed Student Success: General Education and Occupational Programs." *Community College Review,* 1991, *19,* 14–23.

Nora, A. 2000. *Reexamining the Community College Mission.* Washington, D.C.: American Association of Community Colleges, 2000.

Oregon University System and Oregon Department of Community Colleges and Workforce Development. *Students Who Transfer Between Oregon Community Colleges and*

Oregon University System Institutions: What the Data Say. Eugene: Oregon University System and Oregon Department of Community Colleges and Workforce Development, 2000.

Palmer, J. C. "The Characteristics and Education Objectives of Students Served by Community College Vocational Curricula." *Dissertation Abstracts International,* 1987, *48,* 2794A.

Phillippe, K. *National Profile of Community Colleges: Trends and Statistics.* (3rd ed.) Washington, D.C.: Community College Press, 2000.

Prager, C. "The Other Transfer Degree." In C. Prager (ed.), *Enhancing Articulation and Transfer.* New Directions for Community Colleges, no. 61. San Francisco: Jossey-Bass, 1988.

Shearon, R. W., Brownlee, I. A., and Johnson, D. N. *Student Diversity and the Emerging Workforce: The Changing Profile of Students in North Carolina Community Colleges.* Raleigh: Department of Adult and Community College Education, North Carolina State University, 1990.

Striplin, J. C. "ERIC Review: An Examination of Non-Liberal-Arts Course Transferability in California." *Community College Review,* 2000, *28,* 67–78.

Townsend, B. K. (ed.). "Understanding the Impact of Reverse Transfers upon the Community College." New Directions for Community Colleges, no. 106. San Francisco: Jossey-Bass, 1999.

Townsend, B. K., and Ignash, J. "Assumptions About Transfer Behavior State-Level Articulation Agreements: Realistic or Reactionary?" Paper presented at the annual meeting of the Association for the Study of Higher Education, Sacramento, Calif., 2000.

Witt, A. A., Wattenbarger, J. L., Gollattscheck, J. F., and Suppiger, J. E. *America's Community Colleges: The First Century.* Washington, D.C.: American Association of Community Colleges, 1994.

BARBARA K. TOWNSEND *is professor of higher education and associate dean for research and development at the University of Missouri-Columbia.*

7

The new vocationalism has spread the concept of work-based learning into new technical areas and to new student populations. This chapter describes how a new manufacturing technology program at one college, seeking to use work-based learning extensively, has addressed success factors identified in a national study of exemplary programs.

Work-Based Learning: Finding a New Niche

George H. Johnston

Cooperative education, apprenticeship, internship, clinical, school-based enterprise, youth apprenticeship, work-based learning, school-to-work, education to careers: by whatever name it is called, education that takes place outside the normal classroom setting is, and has been for some time, a critical component of how some students learn. As Stern and Rahn (1995) put it, work-based learning (WBL) is essential to career-related education models. This chapter explores some of what is known about WBL, particularly how previous research on the topic can be used to expand into new niches to meet emerging community needs better. Specifics are provided about how one community college in east-central Illinois recently developed a new apprenticeship program in manufacturing technology.

Two primary reasons have been advanced for WBL: "(1) to create and sustain effective workforce preparation systems and (2) to improve teaching and learning practices" (Bragg and Hamm, 1996, p. 10). The economic argument for developing and improving workforce preparation has been widely circulated and reported, including the relationship between poor academic preparation and low technical skills among recent high school graduates (Nothdurft, 1989; Jobs for the Future, 1990, 1991; U.S. Department of Education, 1991, 1993).

Critics of WBL complain that new school-to-work initiatives are undermining new higher academic standards. Hughes, Moore, and Bailey (1999) assert that claims of academic reinforcement are likely developed as an "apt rejoinder" (p. 2) to such criticism. However, they studied five WBL programs in depth and concluded that "work-based learning proponents who stand on the reinforcement claim as a way to convince skeptics of the program's value are standing on thin ice" (p. 36). They went on to argue that "there are other, non-academic but equally important forms of learning that can come from work experience and that these forms give us good grounds for supporting work-based learning—when it is done well" (pp. 35–36).

Lessons Learned from Prior Research

In 1994–1995 a team of researchers associated with the National Center for Research in Vocational Education (NCRVE) and the National Council for Occupational Education (NCOE) developed research protocols and conducted in-depth case studies of ten programs thought to be exemplary at eight two-year colleges (Bragg and Hamm, 1996). The researchers identified a number of factors that seemed to contribute to the success of exemplary WBL programs (Bragg and Hamm, 1996):

Strong program leadership—clearly identified champions willing to work hard and make a visible commitment to keep the programs vigorous

Exclusive connection with the local environment (a niche market)—closely connected to local markets where programs are perceived as having a direct impact on the local economy

Frequent communications with local employers—both formal and informal communication mechanisms involving college personnel and employers and employees

Beliefs about program excellence—a cultural phenomenon that perpetuates a positive reputation that must be monitored

An effective school-based learning component—curriculum maintained within the mainstream of the institution, supported by upper-level college administrators, and connected to WBL

Adequate and diverse financial support—long-term planning to ensure that WBL programs are well funded from a variety of sources, including the private sector

Innovative program and pedagogical features—multiple teaching and learning systems including structured individualized learning plans for student success, workplace mentoring, and articulation agreements

Bragg and Hamm (1996) also noted concerns: "problems can occur in the delivery of work-based learning in two-year colleges" (p. 51). These problems include fears that employers may have about increased liability risks, the need to provide adequate training to prepare employers to become more effective mentors, and the need for colleges to be prepared to take on the very time-consuming responsibilities that are inherent in this mode of instruction. In addition, the authors found three specific issues that did not emerge until the later phase of the study: an apparent preference for adult workers, particularly with respect to tech prep students and youth apprenticeships; concerns that employers were taking the best students; and the feeling that WBL programs were too long, making too many demands on students.

As a member of the NCRVE/NCOE research team, I am now involved in a follow-up study of the ten programs to determine changes that have taken place. Although this study is incomplete, some preliminary observations can be shared to assist two-year college administrators who are considering expanding their WBL offerings. In fact, our initial follow-up results are promising: most of the WBL programs have continued, and some have expanded into related fields, finding a secondary niche market.

Work-Based Learning at Parkland College

A specific example of how administrators and faculty have been informed by research can be found by looking at one community college's attempts to expand its WBL offerings. Parkland College is located in east-central Illinois. The largest county in the district, Champaign, contributes approximately 70 percent of the students who enroll at the college and has approximately 40 percent of the total population for the twelve counties in the college's district. Champaign County enjoyed low unemployment each year from 1990 to 1999. The unemployment rate in that period was also significantly less than the national average and lower than the average for the state (Champaign County Regional Planning Commission, 1999). In only one of the past five years has unemployment risen above 3 percent. Approximately 85 percent of the nonagricultural jobs in the county are in service-producing categories as compared with manufacturing jobs, which constitute the other 15 percent.

Following preliminary reports of the WBL studies done for NCRVE/NCOE, administrators at Parkland College expressed an interest in expanding their WBL programs. Since 1996, ten new courses with a work-based component have been added. The college, located in a mostly rural area, always had a vigorous work-based component (unpaid clinical) in its health occupation programs, and several other programs had work-based courses (paid internships), including construction technology and automotive technology.

In 1968–1969, Parkland began a program in mechanical technology that eventually evolved into what is now known as the manufacturing technology program (MFT). The original program had never had large numbers (fewer than ten degree-seeking students between 1986 and 1990) and did not have a WBL component, although a simulation of a production facility was attempted. The equipment in the labs was largely World War II vintage lathes and drill presses designed for metalworking. When the long-time, sole faculty member in MFT retired, no full-time replacement was hired, causing declines in the program. Several attempts had been made to revive the program through the development of dual-credit tech prep activities with three local high schools, but the attempts were largely underfunded and no clear relationship with area manufacturers was evident.

By the mid-1990s, senior administration was under considerable pressure from local manufacturing companies to improve and expand the nearly defunct MFT program significantly. In 1995, Parkland's president approached a local high school vocational faculty member, who was also a part-time welding instructor at the college, to see if he would be interested in working full time to develop a new and improved MFT program. A technology roundtable composed of representatives from thirty-six local manufacturing firms met to develop a curriculum that would have WBL as a major component. A seventy-credit-hour program was agreed to, with twelve of those hours being work based. Lab equipment was updated to take advantage of computer numerical controls, as well as hydraulics, pneumatics, and plastics for industry.

The technology roundtable, along with faculty members from the college's engineering science and technologies department, met often to develop a set of clear responsibilities for the college, the program director, the students, and the manufacturing sponsor. The college agreed to provide dedicated classrooms and labs, hire instructors, maintain student records, and promote the program. The manufacturing sponsor would assist in interviewing and selecting prospective students, appoint a work site coordinator, pay the trainees, and provide student evaluations that reflected the students' accomplishments during their assigned WBL experience.

The students admitted had to be at least eighteen years of age by the time of the first on-site placement (due to liability concerns), be a high school graduate or equivalent, be accepted into Parkland's associate degree program, be sponsored by a manufacturer, and hold a valid driver's license. The student, the sponsor, and a college representative each were required to sign a formal training agreement that bound all parties to certain understandings. These included a WBL experience with a minimum of 320 hours on the job at minimum wage or higher, a trainer from the sponsoring company to assist the student with learning on the job, and a college representative to make instructional visits during the hours of training. The agreement also detailed the process by which the WBL experience could be terminated.

A candidate interview record evaluation form was developed that would be completed by the interviewer for each participating student. This form consisted of five general questions, each with a five-point Likert-type response that ranged from Excellent to Poor. The questions were about appearance, attitude, apparent technical knowledge, communication skills, and interviewing. The interviewer was also encouraged to add comments.

An individualized education training plan was developed that detailed the program activities, departments involved on site, responsibilities, tasks, and objectives that the student would be exposed to during each assigned placement. In addition, the student was expected to keep a journal addressing a minimum of three areas of learning: new skills learned during the term, skills improved, and areas where improvement was most needed in the future.

The original program was modeled after the Ford ASSET (Automative Student Service Educational Training) program, which allows students to get job training at dealerships, but it quickly became apparent that modifications would be needed to fit the Ford model. This is because in the automotive program, students are exposed to a process that is essentially homogeneous; that is, all students experience more or less the same concepts in roughly the same order and at approximately the same time, even though the students are located at different work sites. According to the original program director, MFT covers a much wider variety of activities, and students bring a much wider variety of experiences to the WBL environment. Some have had jobs in an industrial setting prior to starting the MFT program, and others have not. Some work part time and attend school full time, and others work full time and attend school part time.

Initially, the program was begun as a certificate program. In 1997, it was modified and expanded to a two-year associate in applied science degree program. During the first year, twenty-four students enrolled in the two-year program. By the third year, the number of students enrolled had more than doubled to forty-nine in various stages of degree completion. In fiscal year 2000, sixty-eight students were on record as enrolled in one of five manufacturing degree or certificate programs. Nearly all were male, and nearly all were white. Approximately half had graduated from high school prior to 1991. Although only minimum wages are required by the contract, the average hourly wage range reported varied from eight to nine dollars, up to a high of sixteen dollars.

Success Factors and Persistent Concerns

To evaluate the WBL component better, the success factors and issues identified in the study by Bragg and Hamm (1996) proved to be a useful model. Semistructured interviews were conducted with seven faculty and staff members who had experience with the MFT program: the college president, the dean of career education, the department chair responsible for the program, the current program coordinator, two faculty members, and one employer. Several themes emerged from the interview sessions:

• *Strong program leadership.* The importance of hiring the right person to head up WBL programs cannot be overstated. As one interviewee put it, "It's not enough to have someone who knows the subject. It's not enough to have someone who can teach the subject. You must have someone who can sell the program. Someone with a fire in their belly for manufacturing."
• *Exclusive connections between the program and its environment (niche market).* One of the biggest concerns reported by the department chair was "to keep manufacturers off the backs of the students so that they could complete the program." Apparently, students were occasionally enticed by their supervisors to drop out of the MFT program and work full time. Manufacturers are

still unable to find enough new employees from this program and report the need to recruit from outside the college district.

• *Frequent and effective communications with local employers.* From the very beginning of the discussions about revamping the MFT program, senior administration played a critical role in establishing a close working relationship with local employers. When asked what other chief executive officers needed to know about moving into new niche markets, the college president replied, "Be certain to bring in the top leadership from the local companies—people who have the authority to make things happen. Don't get defensive. Listen. Acknowledge that there may be a need to change. Identify a champion who will devote his [sic] or herself to do whatever it takes to make the program happen." The president also suggested that local employers, with their knowledge of industry needs, had served as a valuable source for part-time faculty.

• *Beliefs about program excellence.* Several of those who were interviewed reported that they believed the MFT program was quite good, but the program is probably too new to have developed intense loyalties seen in programs identified by Bragg and Hamm (1996).

• *Effective school-based learning component.* The MFT program is maintained within the Department of Engineering Science and Technologies. Faculty (full and part time) are hired and evaluated by that department's chair. The majority of the hours required for graduation (fifty-eight of seventy credit hours) are taken in a school-based context. The program appears to have the support of senior administration. All programs (career and transfer) at Parkland are normally reviewed on a five-year cycle. MFT is currently being reviewed, but that process has not yet been completed.

• *Adequate financial support.* Manufacturing partners made possible the purchase of very expensive equipment at large discounted prices. Nevertheless, there seemed to be some resistance from other faculty members in the department about one program's absorbing so much of relatively limited resources. In fact, dollars for new equipment were actually spread among the various other programs in the department. Thus, all programs shared from the increase in support.

• *Innovative program and pedagogical features.* An important element in the program is the use of individualized student plans. Such plans enable the program director to have some influence over how the employer uses the student. According to the program director, employers tend to use students to meet specific needs at the time rather than consider the needs of student workers. No specific innovative features were identified.

• *Other issues.* One of the concerns that Bragg and Hamm (1996) identified was the effect of "creaming," which might be understood several ways. In the original study, there seemed to be some concern that local employers might not always share the college's commitment to diversity and access, and so only certain students might be allowed to participate in WBL activities. A variation on that concern was also expressed by several faculty members who were interviewed. The concern was that part-time faculty might be using class rosters for recruitment information for the companies they represent.

Conclusion

Based on these preliminary results, several observations seem in order. In Parkland's MFT program, many features required to create an effective new WBL program are in place: strong ties with local industry, strong commitment from senior administration, and pedagogical features from exemplary programs. There could be stronger financial support, but there was no evidence that limited resources were holding the program back. Still, one essential item seems to be missing: students. To date, students have not enrolled in sufficient numbers to make the program viable. For each of the past two years, the number of new students entering the program has declined, despite efforts to increase recruitment efforts, including hiring a full-time recruiter. In fall 2000, there were only thirteen new students in the program; this number is barely above the minimum of twelve required to offer the class and substantially below the maximum available slots of twenty-four.

It is ironic that a program that has had successful outcomes and a clear local demand for new graduates has been unable to attract students. One of the dangers of opening a new niche market seems to be that extraordinary efforts are needed to overcome the natural lack of awareness of the industry. In an environment where friends, neighbors, and relatives are not employed in the field, the community may not be responsive to market needs regardless of the quality of the program. As the college president put it, "This is not a field of dreams. Just because you build it doesn't mean they will come."

References

Bragg, D. D., and Hamm, R. E. *Linking College and Work: Exemplary Policies and Practices of Two-Year College Work-Based Learning Programs*. Berkeley: National Center for Research in Vocational Education, University of California at Berkeley, 1996.

Bragg, D. D., Hamm, R. E., and Trinkle, K. A. *Work-Based Learning in Two-Year Colleges in the United States*. Berkeley: National Center for Research in Vocational Education, University of California at Berkeley, 1995.

Champaign County Regional Planning Commission. *Champaign County Statistical Abstract*. Urbana, Ill.: Champaign County Regional Planning Commission, 1999.

Hughes, K. L., Moore, D. T., and Bailey, T. R. *Work-Based Learning and Academic Skills*. New York: Institute on Education and the Economy, Teachers College, Columbia University, Sept. 1999.

Jobs for the Future. *Youth Apprenticeship, American Style: A Strategy for Expanding School and Career Opportunities*. Cambridge, Mass.: Jobs for the Future, 1990.

Jobs for the Future. *Essential Elements of Youth Apprenticeship Programs: A Preliminary Outline*. Cambridge, Mass.: Jobs for the Future, 1991.

Nothdurft, W. E. *Schoolworks: Reinventing Public Schools to Create the Workforce of the Future.* Washington, D.C.: Brookings Institution, 1989.

Stern, D., and Rahn, M. "How Health Career Academies Provide Work-Based Learning." *Educational Leadership,* 1995, *52,* 37–40.

U.S. Department of Education. *Combining School and Work: Options in High Schools and Two-Year Colleges.* Washington, D.C.: Office of Vocational and Adult Education, U.S. Department of Education, 1991.

U.S. Department of Education. *Vocational-Technical Education: Major Reforms and Debates 1917–Present.* Washington, D.C.: Office of Vocational and Adult Education, U.S. Department of Education, 1993.

GEORGE H. JOHNSTON *is director of development, research, and planning at Parkland College, Champaign, Illinois.*

8

Instructional priorities have shifted to accommodate new categories of learners and acknowledge students' multiple intelligences. Constructivist curriculum theories have been employed to meet learners' needs in vocational programs.

Learner-Centered Instructional Practices Supporting the New Vocationalism

Donna E. Dare

Since the early 1900s and the enactment in 1917 of the Smith-Hughes Act, education for work (historically known as vocational education) and education have frequently been viewed as disparate enterprises. Although vocational education has been an increasingly visible and viable part of education over the past half-century, a far more dramatic shift has occurred in the past decade with the implementation and development of such initiatives as tech prep, school-to-work, the Workforce Investment Act (WIA), and certification-oriented programs sponsored by high-tech firms such as Cisco.

These and other educational changes, along with the activities and structures that have accompanied them, have risen like phoenixes from the near ashes of what we have come to think of as traditional vocational education. The activities and structures of these reforms have included changes such as curriculum integration, work-based learning, contextual teaching and learning, and career guidance for all students. As many of these reform activities and structures have been clustered together, they have been coined the *new vocationalism* (Grubb, 1997; Hull, 2000), a term that has come to indicate the highly eclectic nature of new and viable approaches to education for work. These reforms are still fighting battles that are deeply rooted in worn-out perspectives on traditional vocational education. Yet they have gone a long way in addressing the needs of the learners who are now participating in vocational studies in community college classrooms by building on research on cognition and the nature of learners and addressing needed changes in teaching and learning, with a new emphasis on learner-centered instruction.

New Understandings of Learning

Recent years have seen increased efforts in addressing the needs of diverse learners and attempting to make changes in the educational system to accommodate the needs of a more diverse population (Rendon, Hope, and Associates, 1996). As minority populations have continued to grow and as schools have been required to meet the needs of more and more diverse learners, attempts have been made to tackle these issues at least in part on the basis of gender, ethnicity, and economic status. Throughout history, however, our understanding of intelligence and ability has also led to injustices in equity of educational opportunity and has resulted in elitist practices of education that neglect the needs of the majority of learners (Parnell, 1985).

As a result of these perceptions of intelligence and ability, vocational education has also been plagued with inequities in opportunity. Despite the technological demands of the workplace and the increased need for qualified employees to fill the 65 percent of the nation's jobs that are classified as skilled and technical, most students still consider a four-year professional degree program as the "only way to win" (Gray and Herr, 1995, p. xi), and most teachers and counselors gauge their success on how many of their students pursue baccalaureate degrees. In addition, despite the increased rigor of new vocational programs such as tech prep, students of lower ability levels continue to be tracked into these programs because many educators view them as inferior and appropriate only for non–college bound students.

As questions have emerged regarding the validity of traditional perspectives of intelligence (Calvin, 1996; Gardner, 1993; Goleman, 1995; Howe, 1988; Sternberg, 1997), an increasing interest has emerged in the diversity of learners and in how to facilitate students of diverse learning styles and intelligences with the ability to function well in both school and the world beyond. This new perspective of intelligence and potential has introduced a forum for addressing questions of ability and how to nurture that ability through education.

Proposed originally by Gardner (1983), the theory of multiple intelligences closely parallels the concerns of Parnell and others for individual differences among learners and also supports his position on the need for continuity of learning. Multiple intelligences also deemphasize "rote, ritualistic, or conventional performances" and instead place emphasis on "performances of disciplinary (or genuine) understanding," whereby students are enabled to take information and skills learned in school or other settings and apply them in new situations (Gardner, 1991, p. 9). According to Gardner's pluralistic view, multiple intelligence is "the ability to solve problems, or to fashion products, that are valued in one or more cultural or commu-

nity settings" (1993, p. 7). Individuals are viewed as "collections of apti-
tudes" (p. 27) rather than as one-dimensional representations of a single,
measured intellectual capacity. Their capabilities gain value as they are
applied or used in various contexts. Such a definition of intelligence provides a radical view of the complexity and potentiality of learners' "diversity of human ability" (Gardner, 1993, p. 27); it also provides a radical view
of the challenge of the educational system in meeting the learning needs of
such complex and diverse learners.

Gardner (1991) indicated that the ideal educational practice is one that
emphasizes "richly structured activities and projects, students' initiative and
'stake,' constructive forms of learning, and meaningful involvement with the
school and the wider community" (pp. 198–199). According to Gardner,
this type of educational practice leads learners toward understanding rather
than mere acquisition of knowledge (also the concern of Parnell, 1985, Hull
and Grevelle, 1998, and others). The end goal of understanding is for learners to be able to apply newly acquired knowledge in any context—at home,
on the job, or in the classroom.

The critical response to an understanding of the theory of multiple
intelligences is that education needs to structure learning environments in
which learners can move beyond acquisition of knowledge to understanding and applying it. In order to do so, educators need to understand what
those learning environments are and which ones effectively support and
enhance learning and the ability to function beyond the classroom. Thus,
with dramatic changes in the way we look at the potential ability of diverse
learners and with increased understanding of how people construct knowledge, we as educators face new challenges. We are called on to align our
educational strategies to generate optimal learning opportunities for students of all ages with a vast range of intelligences and abilities and a vast
number of pathways they will follow beyond the classroom.

Tech Prep and Integration

A number of terms have been used, both progressively and sometimes inter-
changeably, to identify various strategies employed by vocational educators
during the past decade or so to address the needs of learners and change the
way we deliver instruction to meet those needs. Beginning with the Carl D.
Perkins Vocational and Technology Education Act of 1998 and the implementation of tech prep, a great deal of emphasis was placed on academic
and vocational integration and applied academics. As instructors faced barriers associated with the integration of academic and vocational subject matter and as questions of academic rigor surrounded applied academics,
changes began to occur in how teachers at both the high school and college
levels delivered instruction—with the goal of classroom instruction being
to provide more relevance and rigor in education to meet the increasing
demands of the workforce.

Various approaches have been used to promote relevance in education and a shift from teaching to learning. Perhaps the most difficulty has been apparent in achieving a truly integrated curriculum. Lack of planning time is a serious barrier, particularly in precollege grades. At the postsecondary level, where subject matter expertise is more specialized, the integration of academic content into vocational curriculum or vocational content into academic curriculum may be easier to perpetuate, largely because of a silo or island approach (Grubb, Badway, Bell, and Kraskouskas, 1996). Integration strategies such as infused academic and occupational content, linked or cluster courses, interdisciplinary or multidisciplinary courses, learning communities, work-based learning, technology-enhanced education, and authentic assessment have been advanced as a means of addressing needed shifts from teaching to learning and promoting relevance in education (Illinois Task Force on Academic/Occupational Integration, 1997). Still, attempts at integration at the community college level lag behind secondary integration efforts.

One impetus for change was the introduction of skills identified in 1991 by the Secretary's Commission on Achieving Necessary Skills (SCANS)—a list of competencies desired by business and industry. By viewing the ultimate customer for higher education as the potential employers for graduates of college-level programs, some instructors have been more willing to embrace the inclusion of material and resources that would enable them to teach their own content with a look to what graduates must know and be able to do once they leave the classroom. Where potential employment is a more immediate concern for instructors in some colleges, faculty have often viewed SCANS skills as desirable for all students, and they have revised their curriculum to include work-related skills such as problem solving and decision making.

Academic and Vocational Integration. The integration of academic and vocational education remains a challenging enterprise for college-level instructors, partly because it is such a complex endeavor. Integration can occur on a very low level, such as within-course integration efforts, but it can also occur on a very high level, such as interdisciplinary, team-taught courses or project-based learning. Many instructors include alternate content in their courses but default to within-course integration because they can control what is taught and how the material or content is taught. Cross-disciplinary courses or team-taught courses are more difficult because teachers are required to share responsibility for content. Problem-based or project-based learning can also be more difficult still because it requires that teachers relinquish more responsibility to students or other stakeholders, such as employers. For educators who were trained to be classroom managers and for those who have extensive knowledge and experience, adopting a more learner-centered approach is very challenging. Nonetheless, instructors have found great satisfaction and success in shared approaches to classroom instruction.

According to work conducted by the Illinois Task Force on Academic/Occupational Integration (1997), integration of academic and occupational education, although arduous, is a "task worth striving toward" (p. 17). The task force cited integration as supporting an innovative environment and providing resources that support the shift from a teaching to a learning paradigm. Similarly, Perrin (2000) noted the benefits of integration, including increased faculty motivation, increased intellectual and personal communication, increased collaboration, and improvement in teaching skills and awareness of other disciplines. On the basis of a case study of seven community colleges across the country, Perrin found that integration took shape when there was a faculty person or administrator who served as a champion or had the opportunity to leverage resources that could serve to promote integration efforts.

Unfortunately, integration and associated curriculum changes at the community college level have not advanced nearly as far as their promised potential would indicate or as far as curriculum change at the high school level (Hershey, Silverberg, Owens, and Hulsey, 1998). Whether it is because teachers default to their own resources or because of a strong disciplinary focus, integration at the community college level has remained less than optimum. Some common barriers cited include a focus on teaching rather than learning, lack of contextually based curriculum materials, different standards for the same courses or disciplines, traditional scheduling of courses, faculty workload and union contracts that do not address flexibility in scheduling and the need for planning time, accreditation policies, funding limitations, and a lack of professional development (Illinois Task Force on Academic/Occupational Integration, 1997; Perrin, 2000).

Contextual Learning. According to Hull and Souders (1996), the theory of contextual learning has served as the academic foundation for over one thousand tech prep programs. They defined contextual learning as learning that incorporates recent research from cognitive science recognizing that learning is "a complex and multifaceted process that goes far beyond drill-oriented, stimulus/response methodologies" (p. 15). According to the authors, contextual learning theory allows that learning is enhanced as learners process new information or knowledge within their frame of reference and that the mind naturally seeks meaning in context by searching for relationships that make sense and appear useful. In contextual learning environments, students discover relationships between abstract ideas and practical applications within the context of the real world. Contextual learning theory, as they described it, encourages educators to design learning environments that incorporate as many different forms of experience as possible: social, cultural, physical, and psychological. Contextual learning experiences include the use of curriculum and instructional practices that engage students in relating, transferring, applying, experiencing, and cooperating. According to Hull and Souders, contextually based courses are more interactive, applied, and laboratory oriented than traditional courses are, involve cooperative learning, and require teamwork of all students.

Although cognitive psychologists do not necessarily agree on just how context affects cognitive development, there is at least some consensus that context does play a key role in cognitive development (Berg and Calderone, 1994; Brown, Collins, and Duguid, 1989; Resnick, 1988; Rogoff, 1984; Sternberg, 1994). Because of an interest in the ability of learners to generalize certain aspects of knowledge or skills to new situations (Rogoff, 1984) or to transfer knowledge (de Bono, 1986), research has continued to focus on various means of using context to facilitate learning that will extend beyond the classroom environment or the immediate context. These approaches have included situated learning models (Brown, Collins, and Duguid, 1989; McLellan, 1996), scaffolding (Greenfield, 1984; Rogoff, 1990), cognitive apprenticeship (Collins, Brown, and Newman, 1989), and cognitive mentoring (Schlager, Poirier, and Means, 1996). Although these models deal with the importance of both the individual and the context, or situation, other models focus less on the social contexts for learning and more on cognitive development, the ability of an individual to use knowledge within a variety of contexts over a life span, and the adaptations an individual makes in order to function within specific contexts (Berg and Calderone, 1994). Such models for learning are rooted even more deeply in constructivism as it was prescribed by Bruner (1990). Constructivism, a theory of "learning or meaning-making" (Abdal-Haqq, 1998, p. 1), is based on the notion that learners construct their own understandings or knowledge through the interaction of what they already know and believe and the contexts with which they come into contact (that is, ideas, events, and activities).

Regardless of the evolving terminology, contextual learning provides learners with an understanding of the context for what they are learning, and building on what they know and already understand is a valid approach to teaching and learning. This approach is based on what we know about the way people learn. Promoting relevance can be practiced through a variety of approaches, including scaffolding, cognitive apprenticeships, modeling, and situated learning; all connect learners to the larger context and facilitate their acquisition of both knowledge and understanding. For these approaches to be effective, instructors need to understand them and know how to apply them. Professional development that promotes various methods for more applied approaches to instruction that are rooted in cognitive science should not be abandoned; rather, they should be increased and supplemented so that teachers can continue to build a repertoire of instructional practices that facilitate learning.

How Contextual Learning Works. One shift that must take place in order for instructors to embrace contextual learning is to view content (that is, what must taught) as only part of instructional practice. One model for contextual teaching and natural learning (Zako, 2001) is a four-quadrant

Figure 8.1. Natural Learning Model

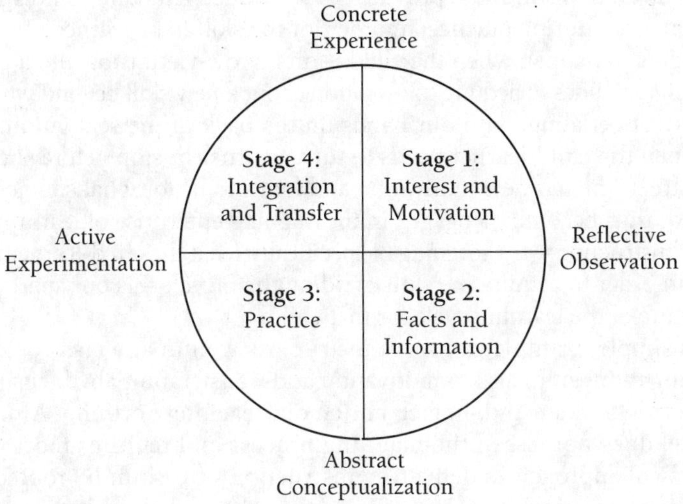

Concrete
Experience

Active
Experimentation

Reflective
Observation

	Stage 4: Integration and Transfer	Stage 1: Interest and Motivation
	Stage 3: Practice	Stage 2: Facts and Information

Abstract
Conceptualization

Source: Zako (2001).

approach that addresses the complexity and dynamic nature of both the teaching and learning enterprises (see Figure 8.1). This model actually deemphasizes the time spent on traditional delivery of facts and information (see Stage 3 in the figure) and emphasizes time spent on other critical elements of the learning cycle: interest and motivation, practice, and integration and transfer. Although the content remains the same and is not compromised, the other factors become part of the plan for delivery of instruction.

This model effectively shifts the focus from the teacher to the learner. In a more learner-centered environment, the content (what must be taught) is also contextualized within the larger scope of engaging the learner in the acquisition of knowledge. Although the plan for the learning cycle remains a primary responsibility of the instructor, more attention is given to drawing the learner into the process. Thus, one-fourth of the process is teaching what must be learned, and three-fourths of the process is geared toward drawing the learners into the process more deliberately—first through motivating them and engaging their interest, then through allowing them opportunities to practice what they have learned as well as to find ways to enable them to make connections between what they have just learned and what they need to learn next.

The simplest example of this process is that of riding a bicycle. As parents-instructors focused on what must be learned, we would talk to a child-learner to explain the parts of bicycle, where to place her feet and hands, and how the bicycle operates. We could explain this process indefinitely, but unless the child-learner wants to learn to ride the bike and has a chance to ride, she will not acquire the ability. The best motivation in this instance might be a playmate down the street who has a new bicycle and has just learned to ride it. We, as parents-instructors, still must provide the assistance, guidance, and specific instruction, even during practice, in order for the skill to be learned. Transferability begins to happen when the child is on her own and runs into a corner or a stop sign and has to acquire information about a new skill beyond what she learns by just pedaling, with our hands on the back of the seat guiding her along. When the child-learner needs to turn a corner or stop before she runs into the street, she has new motivation and looks to us for what she needs to know next, thus becoming engaged in the ongoing enterprise of learning. But the actual instruction—the teaching of specifically what the child-learner needs to know in order to acquire the skill of riding the bicycle—is only part of the larger picture of the learning cycle for that child.

This simple example can serve instructors well in any classroom setting. Giving more emphasis to motivation and transferability by focusing on relevance can broaden and, in fact, enrich our teaching portfolio. Although this model does not lessen the planning process and requires more effort than a typical approach to delivering instruction, it is soundly rooted in a constructivist approach to learning—one based on what we have come to understand about the way people learn.

Promising Results

In a study of youth apprentices in one exemplary tech prep consortium (Dare, 2000), students were asked to indicate the extent to which certain perceived benefits of applied academics were pertinent to them as learners. One of the benefits they identified was the use of different teaching methods that they felt were effective in promoting learning, including putting knowledge in context, applying knowledge to the real world, modeling, actively engaging the learner, and using additional equipment and resources beyond the textbook. Although the participants did not use the term *integration* to describe the methods they considered effective, their descriptions indicated that they frequently used integration strategies they considered to be effective in these learning environments.

Similarly, in the national study of tech prep conducted by Bragg and others (1999), several consortia were engaged in integration strategies based in current understanding of learning theories. For example, although one large state highly engaged in tech prep did not use the term *applied* for its courses, it did encourage infusing real-world applications into traditional academic courses as a means of engaging students in contextual learning. Another consortium emphasizes the new interdisciplinary courses, referred to as Great Thinkers courses, by connecting the theories of prominent scholars and philosophers to modern technological applications, with writing and public speaking a prominent aspect of the learning.

Building more on social aspects of learning contexts, one of the newer innovations in community college instructional strategies is the emergence of learning communities. Learning communities restructure curriculum in a variety of ways to link a cohort of students who participate in a common core of courses during their college experience. By promoting a sense of community and connectedness as part of the educational experience, faculty engaged in learning communities attempt to enhance student success and retention. Although the format is defined by local institutions, a wide range of learning communities has been fostered and perceived as effective in promoting student success and retention. Many students in vocational programs are involved in learning communities in community colleges across the country. Emphasizing the value of community, learning communities also include inter- or multidisciplinary opportunities to learn.

Conclusion

Though prominent in the history of vocational education, legislative initiatives do not offer a panacea for all educational ills. Similarly, no one educational strategy like academic and vocational integration will meet the needs of all learners or all instructors. In addition, no single theory of learning and no single learning strategy will allow us to address adequately the incredibly complex nature of learners and the incredibly complex dynamic of instructional delivery. However, current trends in the new vocationalism and community college reform do provide a context for reexamining the role of education in the development of the diverse learners who enter community college programs. Reexamination must include a reaffirmation of our long-held societal principle that education is a democratic enterprise—based not on gender or ethnicity or socioeconomic status but rather on the nature of learners with multiple intelligences and abilities.

Although questions surrounding the issue of the purpose of education are not new, educators are still divided in their philosophical perspectives of education and its value. Is education valuable and valid for its own sake, or is it valuable and valid only within the larger context as a means of preparing all learners for the world of work beyond the educational system? As tech prep and other reform efforts have attempted to bridge the gap between school and work, between educational institutions and the world beyond those walls, they have effectively set the stage for us to understand that all learning is learning for work on some level and that we as community college educators are all engaged in that enterprise. Promoting relevance in learning by connecting college education to the community beyond the walls of our institutions continues to open windows of opportunity for doing our job differently and far more effectively.

References

Abdal-Haqq, I. *Constructivism in Teacher Education: Considerations for Those Who Would Link Practice to Theory*. Washington, D.C.: Office of Educational Research and Improvement, Dec. 1998. (ED 426 986.)

Berg, C. A., and Calderone, K. S. "The Role of Problem Interpretations in Understanding the Development of Everyday Problem Solving." In R. J. Sternberg and R. K. Wagner (eds.), *Mind in Context: Interactionist Perspectives on Human Intelligence.* New York: Cambridge University Press, 1994.

Bragg, D. D., and others. *Tech Prep Implementation and Preliminary Outcomes for Eight Local Tech Prep Consortia.* Berkeley: National Center for Research in Vocational Education, University of California at Berkeley, 1999.

Brown, J. S., Collins, A., and Duguid, P. "Situated Cognition and the Culture of Learning." *Educational Researcher,* 1989, *18,* 32–42.

Bruner, J. *Acts of Meaning.* Cambridge, Mass.: Harvard University Press, 1990.

Calvin, W. H. *How Brains Think: Evolving Intelligence, Then and Now.* New York: Basic Books, 1996.

Collins, A., Brown, J. S., and Newman, S. E. "Cognitive Apprenticeship: Teaching the Crafts of Reading, Writing, and Mathematics." In L. Resnick (ed.), *Knowing, Learning, and Instruction: Essays in Honor of Robert Glaser.* Hillsdale, N.J.: Erlbaum, 1989.

Dare, D. E. "A Case Study of Applied Academics from the Perspective of Students." Unpublished doctoral dissertation, University of Illinois at Urbana-Champaign, 2000.

de Bono, E. "The Practical Teaching of Thinking Using the CORT Method." In M. Schwebel and C. A. Maher (eds.), *Facilitating Cognitive Development: International Perspectives, Programs, and Practices.* New York: Haworth Press, 1986.

Gardner, H. *Frames of Mind: The Theory of Multiple Intelligences.* New York: Basic Books, 1983.

Gardner, H. *The Unschooled Mind: How Children Think and How Schools Should Teach.* New York: Basic Books, 1991.

Gardner, H. *Multiple Intelligences: The Theory in Practice.* New York: Basic Books, 1993.

Goleman, D. *Emotional Intelligence.* New York: Bantam Books, 1995.

Gray, K. C., and Herr, E. L. *Other Ways to Win: Creating Alternatives for High School Graduates.* Thousand Oaks, Calif.: Corwin Press, 1995.

Greenfield, P. M. "A Theory of the Teacher in the Learning Activities of Everyday Life." In B. Rogoff and J. Lave (eds.), *Everyday Cognition: Its Development in Social Context.* Cambridge, Mass.: Harvard University Press, 1984.

Grubb, W. N. "Not There Yet: Prospects and Problems for 'Education Through Occupations.'" *Journal of Vocational Education Research,* 1997, *22,* 77–94.

Grubb, W. N., Badway, N., Bell, D., and Kraskouskas, E. *Community College Innovations in Workforce Preparation: Curriculum Integration and Tech Prep.* Mission Viejo, Calif.: League for Innovation in the Community College, 1996.

Hershey, A. M., Silverberg, M., Owens, T., and Hulsey, L. K. *Focus for the Future: The Final Report of the National Tech Prep Evaluation.* Princeton, N.J.: Mathematica Policy Research, 1998.

Howe, M.J.A. "Context, Memory and Education." In G. M. Davies and D. M. Thomson (eds.), *Memory in Context: Context in Memory.* New York: Wiley, 1988.

Hull, D. *Education for a New Millennium.* Waco, Tex.: CORD, 2000.

Hull, D., and Grevelle, J. *Tech Prep the Next Generation.* Waco, Tex.: CORD Communications, 1998.

Hull, D., and Souders Jr., J. C. "The Coming Challenge: Are Community Colleges Ready for the New Wave of Contextual Learners?" *Community College Journal,* 1996, *67,* 15–17.

Illinois Task Force on Academic/Occupational Integration. *Blurring the Lines: Integrating Academic and Occupational Instruction at the Community College.* Springfield: Illinois Community College Board, Oct. 1997.

McLellan, H. "Epilog: Situated Learning in the Context of Paradigms of Knowledge and Instruction." In H. McLellan (ed.), *Situated Learning Perspectives.* Englewood Cliffs, N.J.: Educational Technology Publications, 1996.

Parnell, D. *The Neglected Majority.* Washington, D.C.: Community College Press, 1985.

Perrin, D. "Curriculum and Pedagogy to Integrate Occupational and Academic Instruction in the Community College: Implications for Faculty Development." *CCRC Brief,* 2000, *8*, 1–4.

Rendon, L. I., Hope, R. O., and Associates. *Educating a New Majority: Transforming America's Educational System for Diversity.* San Francisco: Jossey-Bass, 1996.

Resnick, L. "Learning in School and Out." *Educational Researcher,* 1988, *16*, 13–20.

Rogoff, B. "Introduction: Thinking and Learning in Social Context." In B. Rogoff and J. Lave (eds.), *Everyday Cognition: Its Development in Social Context.* Cambridge, Mass.: Harvard University Press, 1984.

Rogoff, B. Apprenticeship in Thinking: Cognitive Development in Social Context. New York: Oxford University Press, 1990.

Schlager, M. S., Poirier, C., and Means, B. M. "Mentors in the Classroom: Bringing the World Outside In." In H. McLellan (ed.), *Situated Learning Perspectives.* Englewood Cliffs, N.J.: Educational Technology Publications, 1996.

Sternberg, R. J. "Commentary: Reforming School Reform: Comments on Multiple Intelligences: The Theory and the Practice." *Teachers College Record,* 1994, *95*, 561–569.

Sternberg, R. J. "What Does It Mean to Be Smart?" *Educational Leadership,* 1997, *54*, 20–24.

Zako, W. *Contextual/Natural Learning: Creating "Natural" Learning Environments.* [www.humanptions.com/learning.html]. May 2001.

DONNA E. DARE is tech prep coordinator at Richland Community College, Decatur, Illinois.

9

Although the Workforce Investment Act has reached the implementation stage, questions about its impact on community colleges remain. Interesting and creative work in line with the new vocationalism has been initiated on behalf of low-income clients, but it is still unclear how well community colleges will meet client needs within the framework of the legislation.

Community Colleges and the Workforce Investment Act: Promises and Problems of the New Vocationalism

James Jacobs

On July 1, 2000, the new Workforce Investment Act (WIA) dramatically altered the federal system of job training and workforce development. Although all of the dimensions of the act are still unfolding in voluminous regulation memos and training guidance agreements, the broad outlines of this $5 billion legislation are in place (Visdos, 2000a). For community colleges, WIA marks an important policy watershed. Never before has such a large and comprehensive federal law been created assuming the participation of community colleges. Indeed, through almost all aspects of WIA, from the drafting of the legislation to the current issues over implementation, American community colleges have been considered a critical factor in the success of this legislation.

Indeed, some have argued that passage of the WIA legislation would permit community colleges to use the full array of their resources. Often referred to as the new vocationalism, this approach combines academic and technical education to provide individuals with skill sets not only for entry-level occupations but to pursue careers in high-wage, high-skill occupations. The goal of this approach is long-term preparation for careers, not simply quick, short-term preparation for entry-level jobs. The features of the new vocationalism are especially important in the preparation of low-income citizens for more economically secure employment.

What emerges from the review of the WIA legislation in this chapter is the lack of realization of many of the features of the new vocationalism in

NEW DIRECTIONS FOR COMMUNITY COLLEGES, no. 115, Fall 2001 © John Wiley, & Sons, Inc.

the implementation of WIA. Resources and creativity that community colleges might contribute to the new vocationalism have sometimes been thwarted or blocked by state government plans that continue to emphasize short-term job training for entry-level work.

Initial Impact of WIA

At this writing, WIA is barely one year old, having begun on July 1, 2000. In many aspects, WIA plays to the strength of community colleges because of the longstanding commitment of these schools to educating all members of their communities. The American Association of Community Colleges views WIA as a primary means of broadening educational programs and services for adults, regardless of their economic circumstances (American Association of Community Colleges, 1998). To some extent, WIA targets the same constituencies that community colleges have traditionally served: adults who want to improve their employment and economic status (Levin, 2000). Community colleges are uniquely positioned as gatekeepers for local subbaccalaureate labor markets. Whereas high schools are often unable to develop sustained ties with employers and four-year colleges concentrate on baccalaureate degrees, the comprehensive mission of community colleges makes them readily able to contribute to this important sector of the economy.

Most individual services associated with WIA are focused on ensuring that American citizens become better able to cope with the changing demands of the labor market. Complementary to the basic tenets of the new vocationalism, there is growing recognition that some high-paying careers require more education than a high school diploma but less than a four-year degree. Furthermore, there is greater realization that many skilled jobs are found among small- and medium-size firms (Rosenfeld, 1995). These firms are often invisible in local labor markets, yet when aggregated, they can play a major role in local and regional economies. In comparison to the health care industry, which is heavily licensed, and unionized industries, which are bound by bargaining contracts, small- and medium-sized firms employ persons with job skills highly specific to their industry and the local labor market. Often they are so specialized that the technical knowledge and skills are learned on the job and within the sector, not outside it. Moreover, these firms, often operating without human resource departments, hire small numbers of subbaccalaureate workers, and those hired are rarely unknown to the firm because referrals by family members or friends are the primary way new employees are hired (Grubb, 1996a).

Attempting to deal with the subbaccalaureate labor markets, WIA encourages firms to communicate their labor needs through local workforce development boards. These boards can provide a vehicle to realize mutually beneficial processes of education and training to develop talent within the community. Operating locally, WIA supports national activities such as the establishment of a labor exchange, as with America's Job Bank, and a new national database of training providers, as with America's Learning Exchange, to serve every working adult. Local organizations, including community colleges, can use these services to retrain and develop the local workforce. Indeed, one goal of the system's designers is to encourage community colleges to play a major role in the new workforce system. A joint report from the Departments of Commerce, Labor, and Education recognizes that community colleges are vital to overall efforts in establishing an entire system of workforce development, stating: "Educational institutions also have an important role in educating and training the workforce, not only independently, but also as vendor employers who seek outside providers of training. Community colleges play a particularly important role in adult education as they have often geared toward educating an older, working population" (U.S. Department of Commerce and others, 1999, p. 13).

Governance of WIA involves a multilayered strategy. WIA is administered through a state plan, which itself is administered locally through a coordinated function of the workforce development boards. These boards must comprise individuals from the private sector and others who are stakeholders in the development of the system. WIA explicitly states that community colleges must be represented on the state boards. Because most community colleges are already committed to workforce development and economic development, they can become a natural conveyor of the new local workforce development system. In addition, many local firms have direct experience with community colleges through prior partnerships.

Finally, an important part of the intent of the WIA legislation is the integration of the assessment, career counseling, job search, and training functions. Instead of having separate programs, WIA intends to integrate and deliver services seamlessly through one-stop centers. In theory, if not practice, these centers often parallel programs and services already offered by community colleges, making them an obvious headquarters for the one-stop centers.

Thus far, community college leaders have given significant support to WIA. The new president of the American Association of Community Colleges, George Boggs, has observed, "We [community colleges] have played a strong role and we must continue to do that. It is an important part of the community college mission and part of our economic development role" (Visdos, 2000b). Building on their strengths, community colleges across the country have begun to develop programs and services that address the requirements of WIA, thereby serving the low-income citizens this legislation is intended to serve.

Creative Strategies for Low-Income Citizens

WIA and its companion program, Temporary Assistance for Needy Families (TANF), are intended to provide postsecondary education alternatives for the working poor who lack the basic academic and technical skills to function in the new economy (Jacobs, 2000). Indeed, the great expansion of jobs in the past decade has reduced the number of persons living on public assistance, but many of these persons remain employed in low-wage jobs that do not provide adequate wages to sustain a family. Addressing this need, some community college programs, operating with WIA and TANF funds, have begun to provide the means of lifting persons out of poverty into a sustainable income.

Among the most successful programs is the Bridge Program at the City Colleges of Chicago. This program is an intensive partnership between the community and education designed to help high school graduates make the transition into postsecondary education, increasing their ability to obtain higher-skilled jobs. The program has a variety of partners, including community-based organizations that recruit students and employers who provide jobs. The function of the City Colleges is to develop and deliver curriculum and instruction. Working through one college, this program has been successful in raising the wages of over 125 graduates (Jenkins, 1998). It has also been modified to serve Spanish-speaking Chicago residents and recently expanded into neighborhoods on the west side of Detroit. Funds from local workforce development boards have been used to fund and develop these programs.

Another example of creative use of workforce development board monies is at Shoreline Community College, located in the north Seattle metropolitan area (Jacobs, 1999). This program is designed to attract out-of-school youth, primarily the sons and daughters of low-income families, and help them return to school. Through recruitment by community-based organizations, young people are selected for an intensive program to improve their basic academic skills before they return to regular classes. There is also an employment component that stresses the need for students to develop employability skills. Shoreline Community College runs a program preparing TANF-eligible recipients for careers in specifically targeted high-tech industries in the Seattle area (Jacobs, 1999).

At Cabrillo Community College in a rural California community, career transition services are offered through the Fast Track to Work Office (Golonka and Matus-Grossman, 2001). This office provides special work opportunities and career counseling and financial aid information, along with academic and tutorial support. Many adult students who have engaged in this program have completed their degrees and obtained a job. The strong collaborations operating between the college and local employers have made employment opportunities available to program graduates. TANF funds have contributed to the budget supporting the program.

What makes these three programs successful? First, they are based on goals and services that align training offered by the colleges with the workforce needs of local firms. Partnerships with employers are helpful in addressing various problems of low-income persons, leaving responsibility for the curriculum to the colleges. Second, WIA funds are leveraged with TANF and other program resources to encourage greater coordination and better services for students. Third, these programs are not narrowly focused on specific job training alone; they emphasize dual preparation in academic and technical subjects so that completers are ready to assume employment but are also prepared to continue in college. Fourth, these programs promote better-paying jobs as a means of preparing students for viable careers. In all of these programs, employers play a central role in not only providing clients with jobs but encouraging students to stay in school. Fifth, these programs attract a new constituency of adult students to help their institutions address declining enrollments by working adults. Finally, with the full support of their local leaders, these programs help to fulfill the comprehensive mission of the community college.

Concentrating on addressing the needs of low-income people, community colleges offer several benefits to these individuals. First, low-income individuals gain short-term, job-specific training that is supplemented with basic academic skills that often lead to a certificate or degree. New immigrants can receive English as a Second Language (ESL) training that is contextualized with technical subject matter. In addition, students may have the opportunity to participate in work-based learning, providing them with highly valuable work experience in high-skilled workplaces. When students complete these programs, there are potentially significant economic benefits, including higher income and greater stability in the workplace (Grubb, 2001).

Benefits are evident for the community colleges as well. Because community development is a mission of community colleges, one of the most important services these institutions can perform is to prepare citizens for the new economy. Addressing the skill needs of the working poor makes sense from a community development perspective (Bluestone and Harrison, 2000), and community colleges have a major role to play in preparing people to meet new standards of cost efficiency, quality, customization, and speed (Carnevale and Desrochers, 1997). Community colleges should not only provide customized training for local firms to prepare their incumbent workers, but they should increase the base of skilled workers within the community at large as part of developing and keeping the local infrastructure agile. Armed with better skills, low-income citizens will not only earn more money, but they will be less likely to suffer from the negative economic and social consequences of unemployment.

Having recognized the benefits of community college programs for low-income persons, it is important to note common barriers. Some community college staff oppose efforts to bring WIA- and TANF-funded programs into community colleges because the students they serve are not considered suitable for college. Seen as a drain on traditional programs and services, the relatively high costs of programs and services targeted at low-income citizens may be criticized. Specifically, these programs may strain existing counseling and support services, and these are exactly the kinds of services that are needed to assist students to complete programs successfully.

How WIA Relates to the New Vocationalism

Technical and procedural issues tend to obscure more fundamental issues for WIA. In large part, the success of community colleges in providing students with new careers and jobs occurs because these institutions have mastered the new vocationalism (Bragg, 1997; Grubb, 1997). More integration of academic and technical curricula and instruction and greater emphasis on career ladders are essential, stressing preparation in broad skills that funnel into more job-specific training. This approach does not place students in dead-end jobs, but prepares them for viable career pathways with a future in the new economy.

Community colleges that have made significant progress with WIA appear to have instituted the principles of the new vocationalism, which requires a long-term commitment. WIA programs aligned with the new vocationalism are built on foundational skills that ensure that students can gain access to viable career opportunities. Yet in most state implementation plans, an emphasis on short-term training for low-skill, low-wage jobs predominates. And because many community colleges have not engaged in WIA fully, lessons learned about the new vocationalism have not been incorporated into the system. Positive changes have emerged on the margins but not the mainstream. The new vocationalism is most evident when creative individuals from state agencies and local colleges have collaborated on developing new initiatives. Although these programs are small in scale and often held together by the determination of a committed local administrator, teacher, or counselor, they represent a vision for how WIA funds can be used to sustain significant workforce development initiatives for communities.

Conclusion

It is far too early to judge the impact of WIA on American community colleges. Early problems with implementation have been documented, and the potential for successes is still unrealized. WIA is an experiment in progress. Positive results can be achieved by working with low-income citizens when community colleges focus leadership and resources to meet their needs. Adhering to the principles of the new vocationalism promises to address some of the shortcomings of WIA and serve the needs of more low-income citizens through new WIA-funded programs.

References

American Association of Community Colleges. *The Workforce Investment Act: Implications for Community Colleges.* Washington, D.C.: American Association of Community Colleges, 1998.

Bluestone, B., and Harrison, B. *Growing Prosperity.* Boston: Houghton Mifflin, 2000.

Bragg, D. "Grubb's Case for Compromise: Can 'Education Through Occupations' Be More?" *Journal of Vocational Education Research*, 1997, 22, 115–122.

Carnevale, A. P., and Desrochers, D. M. "The Role of Community Colleges in the New Economy." *Community College Journal,* 1997, 67, 26–33.

Golonka, S., and Matus-Grossman, L. *Opening Doors: Expanding Educational Opportunities for Low-Income Workers.* New York: Manpower Development Research Corporation and National Governors Association Center for Best Practices, May 2001.

Grubb, W. N. *Working in the Middle: Strengthening Education and Training for the Mid-Skilled Labor Force.* San Francisco: Jossey-Bass, 1996a.

Grubb, W. N. *Learning to Work: The Case for Reintegrating Job Training and Education.* New York: Russell Sage Foundation, 1996b.

Grubb, W. N. "Not There Yet: Prospects and Problems for 'Education Through Occupations.'" *Journal of Vocational Education Research,* 1997, 22, 77–94.

Grubb, W. N. "Second Chances in Changing Times: The Roles of Community Colleges in Advancing Low-Skilled Workers." *Workplace,* 2001, 12, 3–5, 20.

Jacobs, J. "Out of School Youth Programs." *Link,* June 1999, p. 1.

Jacobs, J. "Low Income Workers and Community Colleges: A Challenge and Opportunity for NCOE." *Workplace,* 2000, 11, 8–9.

Jenkins, D. "Beyond Welfare to Work: Bridging the Low-Wage-Livable-Wage Employment Gap." Paper presented at the Great Cities Institute, University of Illinois at Chicago, 1998.

Levin, J. S. "The Revised Institution: The Community College Mission at the End of the Twentieth Century." *Community College Review,* 2000, 28, 1–25.

Rosenfeld, S. A. *New Technologies and New Skills: Two-Year Colleges at the Vanguard of Modernization.* Chapel Hill, N.C.: Regional Technologies Strategies, 1995.

U.S. Department of Commerce, U.S. Department of Education, U.S. Department of Labor, National Institute of Literacy, and Small Business Administration. *21st Century Skills for 21st Century Jobs.* Washington, D.C.: U.S. Government Printing Office, Jan. 1999.

Visdos, R. "Have You Read TEGL#7 from the USDOL." *From the Field,* 2000a, 3, 1.

Visdos, R. "Interview with Boggs." *From the Field,* 2000b, 3, 5.

JAMES JACOBS is director of the Center for Workforce Development and Policy at Macomb Community College and associate director of the Community College Research Center at Teachers College, Columbia University, New York.

10

This annotated bibliography presents recent ERIC documents that provide information related to evolving vocational education programs, policies, and practices in community colleges.

Sources and Information: Postsecondary Vocational Education

Jung-sup Yoo

The community college's role in vocational education has expanded beyond training an entry-level workforce. The competitive global economy, new forms of work organizations, and technological advancement are changes that influence postsecondary vocational education. To adapt to changes in the new economy, community colleges are seeking to transform their vocational education programs through curriculum reform efforts represented by integration of academic and vocational curricula, increased linkages with other levels of educational institutions, and strengthened partnerships with business and industry and the community.

The sources presented here examine new approaches to evaluating and improving vocational education and literature related to national policies on vocational education and training. They reflect the current ERIC literature on evolving programs, policies, and practices pertaining to postsecondary vocational education. Most ERIC documents (publications with ED numbers) can be viewed on microfiche at over nine hundred libraries worldwide. In addition, most may be ordered on microfiche or on paper from the ERIC Document Reproduction Service (EDRS) by calling (800)443-ERIC or going to www.edrs.com.

Curriculum Reform Efforts

The following materials provide information on diverse approaches to curriculum reform in community colleges, including integration of academic and vocational curricula and work-based learning experiences.

Bragg, D. D., Hamm, R. E., and Trinkle, K. A. *Work-Based Learning in Two-Year Colleges in the United States*. Berkeley: National Center for Research in Vocational Education, University of California at Berkeley, 1995. (ED 378 446.)

This report investigated the aggregate scope and quality of work-based learning (WBL) in American public community and technical colleges, using data from 454 two-year colleges responding to a mailed survey. An average of 18 percent of students in vocational programs were estimated to participate in WBL in the responding institutions. In addition, approximately one-quarter of the respondents indicated that over half of students involved in customized or contract training were participating in WBL. More than sixty programs were reported to require WBL, and most of these were in the health and business fields. Nursing was the only program that consistently mandated WBL (due to licensure requirements). Nearly all health WBL programs employed the professional and clinical model, and about two-thirds of nonhealth WBL programs used the cooperative education model. WBL experiences were rarely a required component in manufacturing and high-technology programs.

Results revealed that common problems were a lack of resources and a lack of involvement from the business community. To increase WBL experiences in community colleges, recommendations are provided, including more fiscal resources, more incentives for business to participate in WBL partnerships, and clearer standards.

Bragg, D. D., Reger, W., and Thomas, H. S. *Integration of Academic and Occupational Education in the Illinois Community College System*. Springfield: Illinois Community College Board, 1997. (ED 418 757.)

This study investigated diverse practices associated with curriculum integration in Illinois community colleges, using telephone surveys, interviews, and document analysis. Among the forty-four Illinois community colleges responding to the survey, nearly all reported the infusion model of curriculum integration, such as applied academic courses and incorporation of academic content into occupational courses. A few provide linked courses and cluster courses, developed and coordinated by a team of faculty members, and some provide multidisciplinary courses in health, business, and environmental areas. Only a handful had implemented learning communities to integrate academic and vocational curricula. WBL experiences were provided in almost all occupational fields, and these experiences were more intensive when required for licensure and certification. Finally, a growing number of courses use computer applications across the curriculum, especially in mathematics and science.

Grubb, W. N., and Kraskouskas, E. *A Time to Every Purpose: Integrating Occupational and Academic Education in Community Colleges and Technical*

Institutes. Berkeley: National Center for Research in Vocational Education, University of California at Berkeley, 1992. (ED 350 405.)

This technical report explores diverse approaches to, barriers to, and benefits of curriculum integration in community colleges based on data collected through a telephone survey of a randomly selected sample of 295 community colleges and 45 community college officials and field visits to four campuses. The authors categorized curriculum integration into eight distinct approaches: (1) requiring general education for certain occupational students, the most frequent form of curriculum integration; (2) developing academic courses with applications in occupational areas such as technical writing and business math (applied academics); (3) employing cross-curricular models incorporating academic skills in occupational programs such as "writing across the curriculum"; (4) introducing academic modules such as history and ethics into occupational courses; (5) developing multidisciplinary courses combining academic perspectives and occupational concerns such as history of technology; (6) developing tandem and cluster courses that use two or three complementary courses for students to take simultaneously; (7) creating colleges-within-colleges in which a cohort of students take all their courses together; and (8) developing remedial or English as a Second Language courses to teach basic math and English with introductory material in an occupational area. Several barriers to curriculum integration were reported, such as disciplinary specialization, the status difference between vocational and academic instructors, lack of resources for cooperation among faculty members, and lack of leadership for curriculum reform. Increasing student competencies and faculty cooperation were presented as benefits.

Hughes, K. L., Moore, D. T., and Bailey, T. R. *Work-based Learning and Academic Skills.* New York: Institute on Education and the Economy, Columbia University, 1999. (ED 440 263.)

This study investigated the relationship between participation in WBL and academic learning using data gained through interviews with faculty, staff, students, and employers, along with observations of the WBL experiences of students. At three sites, twenty-five student interns were observed several times for several hours each time and interviewed before and after their work placements. The study found no evidence of academic reinforcement in the workplace for nine of the students. For sixteen students, evidence was found for some level of academic reinforcement in the workplace. Seven students showed increased motivation to learn by participating in WBL. Almost half the students experienced that they applied learning in school to their work. The authors concluded that knowledge gained in the workplace could reinforce academic learning, especially if there is intentional instructor intervention connecting school-based learning and WBL. They also claimed that WBL can have positive effects on academic learning when it is done well.

Partnerships with Educational Institutions

The following sources provide insights into community colleges' relation-ships with four-year colleges and secondary schools, particularly in the vocational education area.

Bragg, D. D., and others. *Tech Prep Implementation and Preliminary Student Outcomes for Eight Local Tech Prep Consortia.* Berkeley: National Center for Research in Vocational Education, University of California at Berkeley, 1999. (ED 438 420.)

This study examined implementation and student outcomes of tech prep in eight local tech prep consortia represented by various tech prep models and approaches in urban, suburban, and rural locations of the United States. Data were collected from the following sources: repeated field visits to each con-sortium (totaling over sixty high schools and ten community colleges and four-year colleges) involving more than 300 in-depth personal interviews with over 150 secondary and postsecondary students involved in tech prep; follow-up surveys of about 4,700 students with tech prep participants and non–tech prep participants; and high school transcripts for over 95 percent of the 4,700 stu-dents surveyed and nearly 2,000 college transcripts for those students who matriculated to the main community college in the consortium. For each of the eight consortia, the report provides definitions and governance structures supporting tech prep consortia; articulation agreements and practices between secondary schools and postsecondary institutions within consortia; student transition from secondary to postsecondary education; and student secondary academic preparation in mathematics and vocational program areas. Among the study's overall conclusions were that tech prep and school-to-work have formed productive bonds in some local tech prep consortia; enrollment increases have occurred in tech prep curricula as a portion of the total high school enrollment, ranging from 60 to 250 percent; and more than 70 percent of the tech prep participants had enrolled in some form of postsecondary edu-cation, according to the follow-up survey. Data analysis continues, so these results are preliminary; future reports will detail students' experiences related to tech prep at the secondary and postsecondary levels.

Hershey, A. M., Siverberg, M. K., Owens, T., and Hulsey, L. K. *Focus for the Future.* Princeton, N.J.: Mathematica Policy Research, 1998. (ED 423 395.)

This evaluation describes how effectively tech prep is being implemented and identifies useful implementation practices and challenges. Data were col-lected from surveys of state-level tech prep coordinators and local tech prep con-sortium coordinators; in-depth studies of ten local consortia that involved four site visits of each site; and a follow-up survey of a sample of tech prep partici-pants in selected member high schools (the survey was completed by 61 per-cent of the sample of 799 students). The study found that tech prep concepts were widely introduced throughout the country, evidenced by the creation of more than one thousand tech prep consortia involving about 70 percent of all high school districts and serving about 90 percent of all American high school students. Local tech prep consortia pursued diverse implementation strategies, with enhancing vocational programs the most prevalent approach. About 58 percent of all tech prep high school graduates started some form of postsecondary education by the fall of 1995. Of these, about 55 percent selected two-year colleges, and about 60 percent entered articulated vocational programs in community colleges, representing 19 percent of all tech prep high school graduates. Consortia strengthened local collaborations among secondary schools, postsecondary institutions, and business and industry; increased emphasis on career guidance; and focused on applied forms of academic instruction.

Lynch, R. L., Harnish, D., and Brown, T. G. *Seamless Education*. Athens: Department of Occupational Studies, Georgia University, 1994. (ED 391 101, ED 391 102, and ED 391 103.)

This series of three reports investigates issues surrounding transfer of students with associate of applied science degrees to four-year colleges. The first report, *Seamless Education: Why a System for Transfer in Occupational Education?*, identifies forces that underlie the need to examine seamless education and to realize the transfer of two-year college students who are occupationally oriented. The second report, *Seamless Education: A Regional View of Postsecondary Transfer Policy and Practice,* examines postsecondary vocational programs in which students are readily transferring to four-year colleges. It also characterizes the governance structures of higher education and articulation and transfer in Alabama, Florida, North Carolina, South Carolina, and Tennessee. Results show that transfer in vocational program areas most often occurs in engineering technology areas. Transfer of occupationally specific courses is usually on a course-by-course basis and varies among colleges, even within states.

The third report, *Seamless Education: Barriers to Transfer in Postsecondary Education,* explores the barriers to transfer of credit from community colleges to four-year institutions, with special focus on two-year institutions' vocational programs. Several categories of problems were identified: (1) attitudinal barriers, including perceptions of the professional status of two-year college faculty by four-year college faculty; (2) institutional barriers, including expansion of the mission of two-year colleges in remedial education and contract training; (3) financial and geographical barriers; (4) curricular barriers, including the development of separate associate degrees for vocational and transfer purposes; and (5) structural barriers, including the statewide structure, organization, and governance of public higher education.

Partnership with Business and Community

The following sources provide insights into new roles that community colleges are playing in partnering with business, industry, and community groups.

Dougherty, K. J., and Bakia, M. F. *The New Economic Development Role of the Community College.* New York: Community College Research Center, Columbia University, 2000. (ED 439 750.)

The authors explored the role of the community college in workforce preparation and economic development over the past two decades. The analysis is based on national data on the general economic development role of community colleges and an analysis of this role in five industries: auto manufacturing, apparel making, construction, banking, and auto repair. Information on the relationships between firms and community colleges was drawn from interviews, site visits, and document analysis with academic and policy experts; officials employed by firms, industry associations, and labor unions; and officials and faculty at community colleges. The authors defined the new role as contract training, small business development, and local economic development planning. Factors that promoted the new role of community colleges were the demand by businesses to provide training to upgrade the skills of incumbent and potential employees, government policy to attract and retain industry, and internal motivation of community colleges to respond to the external interests of business and government. Enrollment increases, new sources of revenue, and keeping abreast of business skill demands were identified as benefits for community colleges. However, the authors warned that too much focus on the new role might hamper the traditional role of community colleges in providing civic education, resulting in a deep cultural and organizational divide in the community college.

Vocational Education Evaluation and Program Improvement

Using data and standards from the working world, appropriate assessment procedures have been developed to improve vocational education programs and to ensure their continuation.

Brown, B. L. *Quality Improvement Awards and Vocational Education Assessment.* Columbus, Ohio: ERIC Clearinghouse on Adult, Career, and Vocational Education, 1997. (ED 407 574.)

This ERIC digest is intended to identify applications of standards of quality system awards to the assessment of vocational education at the postsecondary level. The three most prestigious awards recognizing quality improvement in business and industry are the Malcolm Baldrige Quality Award, the Deming Application Award, and the ISO 9000 Registration. By comparing standards for the quality management systems awards to vocational education standards of achievement, the author describes assessment of standards for learning and performance (student and employee) and assessment of education-management processes and designs (school and business-industry). The author contends that criteria for the Baldrige Award can be used to assess the effectiveness of educational institutions in meeting customer needs and expectations. The Deming Prize provides the strategy for using statistical methods to assess vocational education enrollment, completion, recruitment patterns, student progress, and economic benefits. The ISO 9000 Registration identifies established standards as a benchmark for meeting quality requirements. These industry-based skill standards offer a benchmark to help vocational educators improve the quality of their programs.

Grubb, W. N. *Learning and Earning in the Middle: The Economic Benefits of Sub-Baccalaureate Education.* New York: Community College Research Center, Columbia University, 1999. (ED 431 459.)

   This report reviews evidence associated with the economic benefits of attending a community college. Effects of subbaccalaureate attendance are presented in general, for special groups, by field of study, and by type of institution. The study provides results of five states' studies of the employment and wage effects of postsecondary vocational programs using unemployment insurance wage data. In general, substantial benefits are evident for many kinds of postsecondary education, particularly when individuals complete vocational programs, enroll in certain occupational fields, and find employment in training-related areas.

National Policies

These sources provide information on national policies that influence postsecondary vocational education and training.

Florida Community College at Jacksonville. *Workforce Development Legislation: A Guide for Adult Education Instructors, Quality Professional Development Project.* Jacksonville: Florida Community College at Jacksonville, 1999. (ED 439 288.)

   This guide is designed for the professional development of new adult education instructors in Florida by providing implications of the Workforce Investment Act of 1998 (WIA) and the Carl D. Perkins Vocational Education Act of 1998. It provides an overview of the WIA and the Perkins Act and then discusses the impact of Florida's 1998 workforce development legislation on adult education students, instructors, and programs. It also describes how to gather student tracking data, including documenting student progress.

Imel, S. *The Workforce Investment Act: Some Implications for Adult and Vocational Education.* Columbus, Ohio: ERIC Clearinghouse on Adult, Career, and Vocational Education, 2000. (ED 437 553.)

   The 1998 WIA consolidates more than seventy vocational education and training programs, providing states the flexibility to develop streamlined services for incumbent and prospective employees. Postsecondary vocational institutions are required partners in one-stop systems, so being represented among those providing leadership for development of state and local workforce development systems is an important issue. Because individual training accounts mandated by WIA will give adults much more choice in selecting where they will be trained, postsecondary vocational institutions known for their high-quality training will probably benefit from passage of the WIA, whereas institutions lacking such a reputation may suffer.

JUNG-SUP Yoo *is a doctoral candidate specializing in community college leadership and tech prep education in the Department of Human Resource Education, University of Illinois at Urbana-Champaign.*

INDEX

109

SINGLE ISSUE SALE

For a limited time save 10% on single issues! Save an additional 10% when you purchase three or more single issues. Each issue is normally $28^{00}.

Please see the next page for a complete listing of available back issues.

Mail or fax this completed form to: Jossey-Bass, A Wiley Company
989 Market Street • Fifth Floor • San Francisco CA 94103-1741

CALL OR FAX

Phone 888-378-2537 or 415-433-1740 *or Fax* 800-605-2665 or 415-433-4611 (*attn customer service*)

BE SURE TO USE PRIORITY CODE ND2 TO GUARANTEE YOUR DISCOUNT!

Please send me the following issues at $25^{20} each.

Important: please include series initials and issue number, such as CC113

1. CC _____

_____

_____

$ _____ TOTAL for single issues ($25^{20} each)

_____ LESS 10% if ordering 3 or more issues

_____

$ _____ TOTAL (Add appropriate sales tax for your state. Canadian residents add GST)

❑ Payment enclosed (U.S. check or money order only)

❑ VISA, MC, AmEx Discover Card # _____ Exp. date _____

Signature _____

Day phone _____

❑ Bill me (U.S. institutional orders only. Purchase order required)

Purchase order # _____

       Federal Tax ID. 135593032   GST 89102 8052

Name _____

Address _____

_____

Phone _____ E-mail _____

For more information about Jossey-Bass, visit our website at: www.josseybass.com